# LONDON'S ZOO

An anthology to celebrate 150 years of
the Zoological Society of London

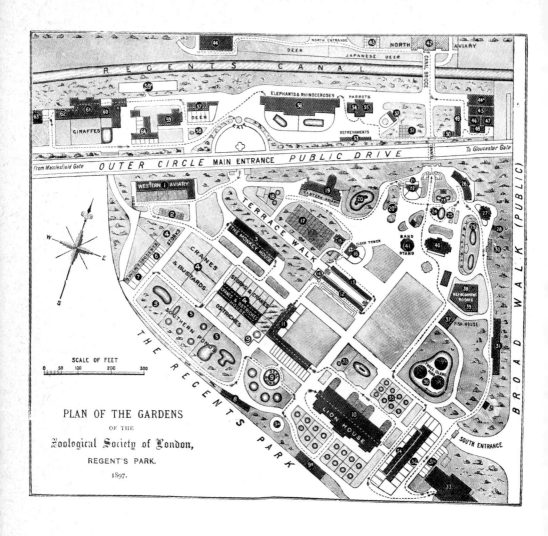

PLAN OF THE GARDENS

OF THE

Zoological Society of London,

REGENT'S PARK.

1897.

# LONDON'S ZOO

An anthology to celebrate 150 years
of the Zoological Society of London, with
its zoos at Regent's Park in London and
Whipsnade in Bedfordshire

COMPILED BY

## GWYNNE VEVERS

zoo (zū). *colloq.* [The first three letters
of ZOOLOGICAL taken as one
syllable.] The Zoological Gardens in
Regent's Park, London; also extended
to similar collections of animals
elsewhere.
*Oxford English Dictionary*

**THE BODLEY HEAD**
LONDON SYDNEY
TORONTO

Printed in Great Britain
for the Bodley Head Ltd
9 Bow Street, London WC2E 7AL
by BAS Printers Limited
Wallop, Hampshire
Set in Monophoto Ehrhardt
First published 1976

# CONTENTS

# INTRODUCTION

An anthology, as the word implies, may be seen as a posy of flowers personally gathered from a well-stocked garden. Any personal selection must show bias and having known the Zoo for over fifty years I plead guilty. Nevertheless, I have tried to select material that will reflect the impact of the animal collections on the visitors and staff who have known the Zoological Society and its zoos and scientific work over the years.

The Society opened the Zoological Gardens in Regent's Park in 1827 and these quickly became popular, not only with the members of the Society—the Fellows—but also with Londoners and visitors from farther afield. For a period in the middle of the nineteenth century the Gardens were perhaps too fashionable. However, alongside its increasing public popularity, scientists in the Society were busy advancing a knowledge of zoology and publishing their discoveries in a series of beautifully illustrated volumes. By the 1860s, and probably earlier, the Zoological Gardens in Regent's Park had become the 'Zoo' to the outside world, a term of affection that has since spread internationally, and is now one of the best-known words in the English language.

One of my early memories of the London Zoo is the opening of the Aquarium in 1924 by King George V, who paused on his way to inspect a particularly impressive orang-utan that lived in the corner of the old Monkey House. About the same time I remember one particular ride on an elephant with Sayaid Ali, the Indian mahout, who was later murdered in the Zoo. It was late in the afternoon one autumn day when my sister and I were given a free ride after the Zoo had closed to the public. We were perched aloft on a howdah, held in by a leather strap, while Sayaid Ali sat astride the elephant's thick neck. Starting from near the old Lion House we were making for the old Elephant House on the other side of the park road, which is now the site of the Clore Pavilion for Small Mammals. This involved riding through the Aquarium tunnel. We had gone perhaps twenty yards when the elephant saw a rat and took fright. It started to stampede and ran straight past the Aquarium and down the tunnel at full speed, my sister and I crouched low on the howdah and trembling with fright. When the elephant emerged at the other end of the tunnel it eventually slackened pace and we reached home badly shaken but unhurt apart from bruises on our backs from the metal frame of the howdah. To this day, I have often wondered what my father, Superintendent of the Society from 1923 to 1948, said to his keepers the next morning.

Many years later, while I was a student, I was able to benefit with practical experience from my father's association with the Zoo: during one vacation I was allowed to dissect a preserved woolly monkey in a laboratory above the Bird House—needless to say I suffered a great deal of nasal irritation from the formalin!

I am particularly grateful to the Zoological Society of London for allowing me complete access to its Archives. The material I have gathered ranges from early nineteenth-century engravings, Council Minutes and other internal documents to numerous volumes of press cuttings going back over a hundred years, and a fascinating collection of black-and-white photographs taken during the first thirty years of this century. Most of these were taken by members of the staff, and in particular by David Seth-Smith, for many years Curator of Mammals and Birds (and also Zoo Man in the late lamented BBC *Children's Hour*), by F.W.Bond, who was the Society's Accountant, and by F. Martin Duncan, a former Librarian. The modern photographs were taken by Michael Lyster, the Society's Photographer, to whom I am much indebted for a great deal of help.

The detail of the jacket illustration is an example of the work of a Bavarian artist, George Scharf, whose lithographs now form a valuable pictorial record of the early days of the Zoo. In 1835 he wrote to the Council of the Society asking for permission to publish lithographic views of the Gardens; this was granted and for many years he sold his illustrations at the gates.

I have made every effort to trace the ownership of copyright material used in this anthology, and both the publishers and myself believe that all the necessary permissions authorizing publication have been granted by authors, agents and publishers. But in the event of question arising over the use of any material the publishers and I, while regretting any error unconsciously made, will be very pleased to make the necessary corrections in future editions of this book. I thank the following publishers for permission to quote extracts from copyright material: William Heinemann Ltd for *Eaglemania*, by

[8]

Jonquil Antony, William Heinemann Ltd and Charles Scribner's Sons for *The Man of Property*, by John Galsworthy; Chatto and Windus Ltd for *A Man in the Zoo*, by David Garnett; Michael Joseph Ltd for *Zoo*, by Louis MacNeice; Hodder and Stoughton Ltd for *The Hidden Zoo*, by Leslie Mainland; Methuen and Co Ltd and McLelland and Stewart Ltd, Toronto for *When we were very young*, by A. A. Milne; Cassell and Co. Ltd for *The Zoological Society of London*, by Henry Scherren, and The Bodley Head Ltd for *The Toys of Peace*, by H. H. Munro.

Where referring to records of the Society, I have abbreviated them as follows: *Minutes* for the Minutes of the Council of the Zoological Society of London, *Annual Report* for the Annual Report of the Council, *Transactions* for the Scientific Transactions of the Zoological Society of London, and *Occurrences* for the daily Occurrence Sheets, which have been kept continuously since 1828.

For general assistance in the compilation of this anthology I am grateful to several members of the staff of the Zoological Society, including Mr R. A. Fish, the Librarian, Mrs Kate Lyster, Miss Joan Ford, and particularly to Miss Unity McDonnell.

GWYNNE VEVERS

# [ 1 ]

# Early Days

'We were then driven to the Zoological Gardens, a place which I often like to visit (keeping away from the larger beasts, such as the bears, who I often fancy may jump from their poles upon certain unoffending Christians; and the howling tigers and lions, who are continually biting the keepers' heads off), and where I like to look at the monkeys in the cages (the little rascals!) and the birds of various plumage.

'Fancy my feelings, Sir, when I saw in these gardens— in these gardens frequented by nursery-maids, mothers, and children—an immense brute of an elephant, about a hundred feet high, rushing about with a wretched little child on his back, and a single man vainly endeavouring to keep him back! I uttered a shriek; I called my dear children round about me. And I am not ashamed to confess it, Sir, I ran.'
*The Sights of London, by W. M. Thackeray, 1850*

# [ 1 ]

# Early Days

A very early press notice
'ZOOLOGICAL, OR NOAH'S ARK, SOCIETY. A public meeting took
place on Saturday last, at the rooms of the Horticultural Society,
at which about a hundred persons were present. Sir Stamford Raffles
was called to the chair, and read an address recommending the
formation of a society, the object of which should be to import new
birds, beasts, and fishes, into this country from foreign parts. The
Regent's Park is to be headquarters; though, if the subscriptions
amount to a sufficient sum, it is hoped that strange reptiles may be
propagated all over the kingdom. But there is neither wisdom nor
folly new under the sun. Worthy Dr Plot informs us, in his History
of Oxfordshire, that King Henry the First enclosed the park at
*Wudestoc* "with a wall, though not for *deer*, but all foreign *wild beasts*,
such as *lions, leopards, camels, lynxes*, which he procured abroad of
other *princes*; amongst which, more particularly, says *William of
Malmesbury*, he kept a *porcupine, hispidis setis coopertam, quas in
canes insectantes naturaliter emittunt, i.e.* covered over with sharp-
pointed *quills*, which they naturally shoot at the dogs that hunt
them." This is the first British National Menagerie that we have
read of: the Romans were much addicted to wild-beast shows.
Considering the advanced state of knowledge, it is to be expected,
that the new Zoological Association will beat both the Romans and
King Henry, in spite of his porcupine; though we do not know how
the inhabitants of the Regent's Park will like the lions, leopards, and
lynxes, so near their neighbourhood.'
*Literary Gazette, 6 May 1826*

This public meeting, held on Saturday 29 April 1826, had been
preceded by much discussion in scientific circles on the advisability
of establishing a living zoological collection in London.

Sir Stamford Raffles was the prime mover, and he was supported
by Sir Humphry Davy, President of the Royal Society and famous
for his invention of the miner's safety lamp, and by many other
'noblemen and gentlemen'.

Raffles was a man of many parts. He spent most of his career in the service of the East India Company, and among his other achievements he was largely responsible for the establishment of the Port of Singapore. He was also passionately interested in natural history and had collected animals during his travels in the Far East. On 9 March 1825 he had written to his cousin, Dr Thomas Raffles, Minister of Great George Street Chapel, Liverpool:

'I am much interested at present in establishing a Grand Zoological collection in the Metropolis, with a Society for the introduction of living animals, bearing the same relations to Zoology as a science that the Horticultural Society does to Botany. The prospectus is drawn out, and, when a few copies are printed, I will send some to you. We expect to have 20,000 subscribers at £2 each, and it is further expected we may go far beyond the *Jardin des Plantes* at Paris. Sir Humphry Davy and myself are the projectors, and while he looks more to the practical and immediate utility to the country gentlemen, my attention is more directed to the scientific department ...

'I sent you by the coach of Saturday a few copies of the prospectus of the Zoological Society. It is a subject on which much has been said, and more might be written, but it has been thought best, in the present state of the speculation, to confine the notice to a few words. The names are coming in fast, and I shall be happy to receive a list of any of your friends at Liverpool who may be desirous of becoming subscribers. The amount of the sum will not ruin them, neither will they find themselves in bad company, and no pecuniary call will be made until the plan is advanced, and we can show them something for their money ... We expect to have at least five hundred members to begin with, and that Government will provide us with ground, etc.'

*The Life of Sir Stamford Raffles, by D.C. Boulger, 1897*

Prospectus of 1825

'ZOOLOGICAL SOCIETY. For the general advancement of Zoological Science, it is proposed that a Society shall be established, the immediate object of which will be the collection of such living subjects of the Animal Kingdom as may be introduced and domesticated with advantage in this country.

'For this purpose a collection of living animals belonging to the Society will be established in the vicinity of the metropolis; to which the Members of the Society will have access as a matter of right, and the public on such conditions as may be hereafter arranged ...

'It has long been a matter of deep regret to the cultivators of Natural History, that we possess no great scientific establishments either for teaching or elucidating Zoology; and no public menageries or collections of living animals where their nature, properties and habits may be studied. In almost every other part of Europe, except in the metropolis of the British empire, something of this kind exists: but though richer than any other country in the extent and variety of our possessions, and having more facilities from our colonies, our fleets, and our varied and constant intercourse with every quarter of the globe, for collecting specimens and introducing living animals, we have as yet attempted little and effected almost nothing; and the student of Natural History, or the philosopher who wishes to examine animated nature, has no other resource but that of visiting and profiting by the magnificent institutions of neighbouring countries ...

'Should the Society flourish and succeed, it will not only be useful in common life, but would likewise promote the best and most extensive objects of the Scientific History of Animated Nature, and offer a collection of living animals, such as never yet existed in ancient or modern times. Rome, at the period of her greatest splendour, brought savage monsters from every quarter of the world then known, to be shown in her amphitheatres, to destroy or be destroyed as spectacles of wonder to her citizens. It would well become Britain to offer another, and a very different series of exhibitions to the population of her metropolis; namely, animals brought from every part of the globe to be applied either to some useful purpose, or as objects of scientific research, not of vulgar admiration ...'

The public meeting of supporters on 29 April 1826 appointed a Council of twenty and elected Sir Stamford Raffles as President. Action was swift. The Council first met on 5 May and again on 30 June. These were the only meetings of Council attended by Raffles, for he died on 5 July at the age of forty-six.

The Society quickly found a house to provide offices at No. 33 Bruton Street, London. A few animals were kept here before the Gardens were opened, not always with very happy results.

'A Report was made by the Clerk that a book of vouchers had been partially destroyed by one of the monkeys kept in the office, which had occasioned a deficiency of 78 vouchers for annual contributions,

comprising the numbers from 101 to 178. It was ordered that a Minute be entered on the Council Book to that effect, and that it be laid before the auditors at the next general audit of the Society's accounts.'
*Minutes, 29 November 1827*

Twenty years later J. W. Broderip, an early member of the Society, recounted an anecdote which possibly refers to the same monkey. 'We have had our eye upon one or two of these Wanderows. There was one in the Zoological Society's collection, then in its infancy, in Bruton Street, and a right merry fellow was he. He would run up his pole and throw himself over the cross-bar, so as to swing backwards and forwards, as he hung suspended by the chain which held the leathern strap that girt his loins. The expression of his countenance was peculiarly innocent; but he was sly, very sly, and not to be approached with impunity by those who valued their head-gear. He would sit demurely on his cross-perch, pretending to look another way, or to examine a nut-shell for some remnant of kernel, till a proper victim came within his reach; then, down the pole he rushed, and up he was again, in the twinkling of an eye, leaving the bareheaded surprised one minus his hat ...'
*Zoological Recreations, by J. W. Broderip, 1849*

The first animals presented
'A letter was read from Joshua Brookes, Esq. communicating his present to the Society of two rapacious birds, viz. the Alpine Griffon (*Vultur fulvus*), and the White-headed Eagle (*Haliaëtus leucocephalus*); and his offer of keeping these birds until the Society's establishment is prepared to receive them. The thanks of the Society were directed to be returned to him for his present.

'A letter was also read from Captn Pearl, of the *Lady Hera*, to the President, announcing his present to the Society of a female deer brought from the Island of Sangor; and the thanks of the Society were directed to be returned to him for his present.'
*Minutes, 5 May 1826*

The Vulture [opposite] remained some forty years in the Zoological Gardens, '... and it is only recently that an old vulture died, that was known to the keepers as "Dr Brookes", as it once belonged to a celebrated anatomist of that name, whose medical school was in

Blenheim Street, Oxford Street, and who was popularly believed to
have kept a number of vultures to consume the mortal remains of
those human subjects that he employed for his anatomical demonstrations. Brookes's medical school was dispersed some forty years
since. The vulture afterwards passed into the possession of the
society; how old it was at that date I do not know.'
*Field, 29 May 1869*

[17]

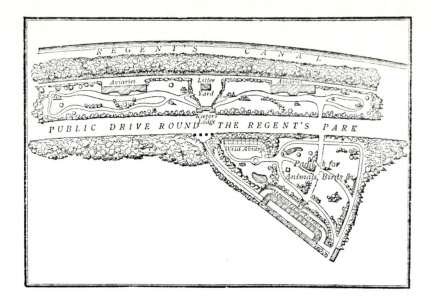

In the meantime the founder members had been looking for a suitable site for the Zoological Gardens. They applied to the Commissioners of Woods and Forests for a lease of Crown land in Regent's Park, and this was granted.

By July 1827 the architect Decimus Burton had prepared his outline for the development of the grounds. The Public Drive shown in his plan [above] is now the Outer Circle of Regent's Park.

The Zoological Gardens were opened in 1827. The first sheet of 'Occurrences' was dated 25 February 1828. These daily records, continued ever since, show how animals were acquired, the progress of building operations, staff matters and visitors' attendances.

Buildings go up at Regent's Park
'Ordered, that the following works be executed at the Garden: Fitting up a stable for zebras, a shed for the kangaroos, a shed for the Indian cows and sheep, replacing the Goat House, a place for the accommodation of the tortoises, preparing accommodation for dogs, an aviary for owls.'
*Minutes, 16 July 1828*

Things begin to happen
'MENAGERIE: Wolf something better. All other animals well.

[18]

Occurrences at the Garden

Monday February 25th 1828

| | |
|---|---|
| Menagerie | Received 11 Wild Ducks, from the Lake caught for the purpose of pinioning & there to be returned — Received 6 Silver Hair'd Rabbits from Mr Blake. Otter died in consequence of a diseased Tail Emue Laid her fourth Egg on 24th Inst All Animals and Birds well |
| Works | Pit for Bear. House for Llama's in progress Boundary wale for supporting the bank next the Bears Pit — begau — |
| Servants | All on duty |
| Number of Visitors | Four |
| Particular Visitor | Lord Auckland |
| Miscellaneous Report | |

E Johnson

Received an Esquimaux Bitch from Mr S.R.Gilbert. WORKS: Pit
for bear. Llamas' House and Boundary Wall in progress. SERVANTS:
All on duty. NUMBER OF VISITORS: Sixty-seven. PARTICULAR
VISITORS: Lord Auckland, Marquis of Lansdowne, Earl of Ilchester,
Major Gen. Hardwicke. MISCELLANEOUS REPORT: Received a
package containing rose trees from Horticultural Society. Lord
Auckland and Marquis of Lansdowne ordered two larger dens to be
made.'
*Occurrences, 3 March 1828*

A favourable press
'GARDENS OF THE ZOOLOGICAL SOCIETY, REGENT'S PARK.
We are again in the Regent's Park; but we must leave its architectural
splendour for the present, and request our readers to accompany us
towards the eastern verge of the Park, to the Gardens of the Zoological
Society, established in 1826, and whose members now amount to
*eleven hundred*! The grounds are daily filled with fashionable company,
notwithstanding the great migrations which usually take place at this
season of the year, and almost depopulate the western hemisphere of
fashion. The Gardens, independent of their zoological attractions, are
a delightful promenade, being laid out with great taste, and the
parterres boasting a beautiful display of flowers. The animals, too,
are seen to much greater advantage than when shut up in a menagerie,
and have the luxury of fresh air, instead of unwholesome respiration
in a room or caravan …
   'Building for Bears, [no. 7] communicating with their pit, (in the
centre of which is a pole with steps for the animals to ascend and
descend). At the extremity of the upper walk, the pit is surrounded
with a dwarf wall and coping, to which (since our sketch was taken)
have been added iron rails. There are here two Arctic bears, and a
small black bear, the latter brought from Russia, and presented to
the Society, by the Marquess of Hertford. There is usually a crowd
of visitors about this spot, and the sagacity and antics of our four-
footed friends ensure them liberal supplies of cakes and fruit, handed
to them on a pole. We were much interested with their tricks, especially
with the vexation betrayed by one of them, at the top of the pole,
when he saw his companion below seize a cake which the former
had previously eyed with great *gout*. His wringing and biting his
paws reminded us of many scenes out of a bear-pit. Then the snorting
and snarling of the old bear below, when the young one attempted to

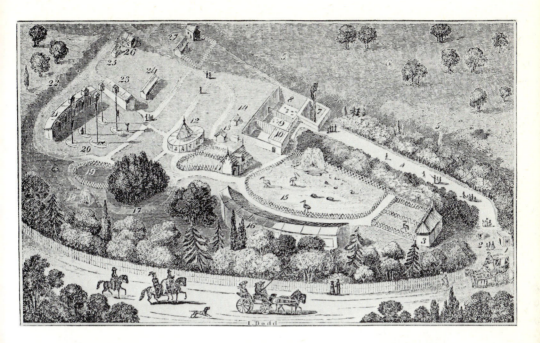

obtain a cake thrown to him; and above all, the small share which our black friend *Toby* enjoyed, probably from his docility over-much,—like good-natured men who are mastered by those of rough natures. We could have stayed here a whole hour, watching their antics, and likening them to the little trickery of human nature ...'
*The Mirror, Saturday, 6 September 1828*

An ailing lynx
'MENAGERIE: Lynx had a convulsive fit. All animals well. Received thirteen carp from Lord Gage. Received a falcon from Mr Stard. WORKS: Pit for bear, Llamas' House and Boundary Wall in progress. SERVANTS: All on duty ...'
*Occurrences, 8 March 1828*

'MENAGERIE: Lynx, still continues unwell, the hinder extremities having been paralytic since the fit of yesterday, gave it an ounce of Castor Oil.'
*Occurrences, 9 March 1828*

'MENAGERIE: Lynx died last evening.'
*Occurrences, 10 March 1828*

'Ordered, that a pair of pelicans offered to the Society by Mr Cragg, of the Honourable East India Company's ship *Atlas*, for the sum of £40, be purchased, if upon inspection they be approved of by the Treasurer and Secretary.'
*Minutes, 18 June 1828*

Gothic house for llamas
'This is one of the most picturesque objects in the grounds. It contains two llamas. These animals are common in South America, particularly in the mountainous parts of Peru, where they are employed as beasts of burthen. One of the llamas was presented to the Society by the Duke of Bedford ...' [An engraving of the house, based on a drawing by James Hakewill, appears below.]
*The Mirror, 6 September 1828*

The Clock Tower added to the Llamas' Hut
(This building, later used for camels, is now scheduled for preservation and animals are no longer kept in it.) 'It was ordered that a clock be prepared for the Garden to be placed on the top of the Llamas' Hut, in an appropriate turret; and that Mr Burton be requested to prepare a drawing of the intended addition to the building for its reception. The expense of the clock and building is not to exceed the sum of £100, including the expense of putting up the same in the turret.'
*Minutes, 18 March 1829*

The Old Tunnel
The Old Tunnel was built to connect the two parts of the original
Gardens. 'Messrs Dickson's specification plan and estimate for the
Tunnel were submitted and approved, and ordered to be executed—
the amount of the estimate being £1,005.'
*Minutes, 16 September 1829*

Fraternal co-operation
'A letter was read from Joseph L. Sabine, Esq., Secretary of the
Horticultural Society, containing an offer, on the part of the Council
of that Society, of supplying the menagerie with fruit and vegetables
from their garden at Chiswick, on payment only of the carriage of
the hampers. The offer was accepted, and the thanks of the Council
were ordered to be returned through Mr Sabine, to the Council of
the Horticultural Society.'
*Minutes, 7 January 1829*

First Indian elephant

The first Indian Elephant walked up from the East India Docks (this method was still used in the present century). 'ZOOLOGICAL SOCIETY. The fine collection of this Society in the Regent's Park has just received a most important addition by the purchase of a noble male elephant, recently arrived from Madras. Preparations have been already commenced for enclosing with a most substantial fence a portion of the Society's garden, as a paddock in which he is to range; and in the centre of which is to be formed a capacious pond for the huge animal to bathe in, an indulgence peculiarly grateful to these animals. The elephant reached the Gardens on the night of Friday week, having walked from the East India Docks in little more than two hours. His paces were so active as to compel the keepers who accompanied him to run frequently, in order to keep up with him. He seemed, indeed, to be pleased at having regained the power of exercising his limbs with somewhat like freedom; and it is rather surprising that he used them so well immediately after quitting the ship in which he had been confined for nine months, having arrived in England by way of China, whither the vessel proceeded after quitting Madras. The elephant took a great liking, when on board of ship, to articles of female apparel; while at Blackwall he took from her head, and devoured without ceremony, a lady's bonnet, and took from another her reticule, containing half a dozen nonpareils, which he swallowed, bag and all!'

*Press cutting, 1831*

Even in this century elephants walked up from the East India Docks to Regent's Park. In 1923 Burmese elephants stroll past Lord's Cricket Ground in the company of Zoo staff.

Admit _____ and Party

TO THE GARDENS

OR MUSEUM OF THE

'ZOOLOGICAL SOCIETY.

*Charles Francis*

*Each Person to pay One Shilling — No admittance on Sundays.*

### Admission by ticket
In the early days the public were admitted only with a ticket from a member and on payment of one shilling—but never on Sundays. Nevertheless, visitors kept coming and in 1829, 199,576 people passed through the gates, and soon there were—

### Plans for a bus service
'A memorial was presented from Mr R.G.Durham, praying for leave to affix a notice in one of the lodges at the entrance to the Gardens, and also in the hall of the house in Bruton St, of his intention to establish an omnibus or other respectable conveyance from Westminster to the Society's Gardens, permission for which was granted.'
*Minutes, 31 August 1831*

But most of the visitors were still the privileged classes. 'The plan of the enclosure at the entrance gate of the Gardens for the accommodation of servants in waiting on the visitors was considered, and it was ordered that one only be at present completed, and that it be a square enclosure. The consideration of the expediency of placing benches in it was referred to the Garden Committee.'
*Minutes, 1 July 1835*

### Traffic problems in the Outer Circle of Regent's Park
'The Superintendent of the Gardens was authorized to obtain

assistance from the police to regulate the carriages at the entrance to the Gardens on Sunday.'
*Minutes, 23 June 1832*

'It was further resolved that a public notice to the following effect be advertised in three morning papers:

'"The Council desirous to prevent as much as possible inconvenience arising to the public from the crowding of carriages on Sundays about the entrance and in the precincts of the Gardens, have given directions to the officers and police in attendance, to prevent any carriages remaining on the south side of the road within 100 feet of the public entrance gates; or to stand otherwise than in single file on either side of the road. And members and their friends are respectfully requested to give orders to their coachmen and servants to attend to the above regulations, and prevent as much as possible the stoppage of the public carriageway of the park."'
*Minutes, 1 June 1836*

Royal co-operation
'The Chairman of the Giraffe Committee submitted a letter from Sir Hubert Taylor, which was read: it announced that His Majesty had been graciously pleased to grant to the Society the use of the Royal Riding House at Pimlico for the temporary accommodation of the expected giraffes on their arrival in London ...

'Mr Sabine was requested to communicate forthwith with the Master of the Horse with a view to facilitate the arrangement which may be necessary for adapting the premises in question for the reception of the animals.'
*Minutes, 20 April 1836*

The popularity of the Zoological Gardens reached its first peak in the late 1830s. 'Within these twelve years past changes, as pleasant to contemplate as they are extraordinary, have taken place in the nature of some of the amusements provided for the people of London. Twelve years ago there stood in the Strand a clumsy awkward building —Exeter 'Change, the lower part of which was a kind of bazaar, the upper a menagerie. This menagerie, and the one in the Tower— both of them very unsuitable repositories,—were all of which the citizens of London could boast as living studies of natural history, at a time when the *Jardin des Plantes* of Paris, under the super-

intendence of Cuvier's master-mind, constituted at once an amusement and a fund of instruction to a vast population. We are fast wiping away the reproach ...

'The zoological gardens in the Regent's Park, for picturesque beauty, far surpass the *Jardin des Plantes* of Paris. They lie on the north-west extremity of London, and in its finest suburban quarter. The gardens are extensive, and their own attractions are heightened by the neighbouring amphitheatre of the Highgate and Hampstead hills. "As we walk along the terrace," says an article in the *Quarterly Review*, "commanding one of the finest suburban views to be anywhere seen, let us pause a moment while 'the sweet south' is wafted over the flowery bank musical with bees, whose hum is mingled with the distant roar of the great city'...

'The engraving [at the head of this page] will give the reader who has not seen the Gardens an idea of the manner in which a small portion is laid out ... A part of the Gardens is separated from the main portion by the road which runs round the Regent's Park; the communication is maintained by a tunnel, which is itself an ornamental object.'

*The Penny Magazine, 16 December 1837*

Detail of an early elephant enclosure from a lithograph of 1835
by George Scharf.

## Promenades

In 1844 the Society instituted Promenade days, reserved for members and their friends, and with the encouragement of a band performance.

The Society's finances were at a low ebb by 1847, and in that year the public were admitted on any week day, except the Promenade days, on payment of one shilling, and they no longer required tickets from a member. In 1848 the charge for admission on Mondays was reduced to 6d, and children paid the same on any day. This was a turning point, and the *Annual Report* for 1850 recorded a great increase in attendances, partly due to the arrival of the first hippopotamus—Obaysch.

The increase in the number of visitors, as compared with 1849, was 191,507, as seen by the following statement.

|  | In 1849 | In 1850 | Increase |
|---|---|---|---|
| Privileged | 33,998 | 59,575 | 25,577 |
| Paying on ordinary days | 51,163 | 117,672 | 66,509 |
| Do. on Mondays | 72,160 | 160,496 | 88,336 |
| Children | 11,574 | 22,659 | 11,085 |
| Total | 168,895 | 360,402 | 191,507 |

*Annual Report, 1850*

# [2]

# Man and
# Zoo

'There had been a morning fête at the Botanical Gardens, and a large number of Forsytes—that is, of well-dressed people who kept carriages—had brought them on to the Zoo, so as to have more if possible, for their money, before going back to Rutland Gate or Bryanston Square. "Let's go to the Zoo," they had said to each other; "it'll be great fun!" It was a shilling day; and there would not be all those horrid common people.

'In front of the long line of cages they were collected in rows, watching the tawny, ravenous beasts behind the bars await their only pleasure of the four-and-twenty hours. The hungrier the beast, the greater the fascination. But whether because the spectators envied his appetite, or, more humanely, because it was so soon to be satisfied, young Jolyon could not tell. Remarks kept falling on his ears: "That's a nasty-looking brute, that tiger!" "Oh, what a love! Look at his little mouth!" "Yes, he's rather nice! Don't go too near, mother."'
*The Man of Property, Book I, Part II, by John Galsworthy, 1906*

'The Wolf Man was in with the wolves. The Mowghli of Regent's Park, as he has been called by the cheaper Press, visits the wolves in no official capacity; he is not on the staff of the Zoo. But because he has a way with wolves, the Zoo, who are all for encouraging our cultural relations with animals, allows him to visit them daily and take a pair of them on chains for an early morning walk round the Gardens.

'The Wolf Man this morning was standing with a steel comb in his hand inside the wolves' cage and talking through the wire-netting to an astonished audience of women. The mother of these wolves had been ill, they had given up hope of her; he asked to be allowed to sit up with her; they said Certainly Not; he offered a letter of indemnity and they said all right, provided it was signed by his wife; then they gave him and the wolf a special room in the Sanatorium; sixty-two hours he sat up with her, it was an absolute fight between Love and Death, but Love conquered, as it always will in this world.'

*Zoo, by Louis MacNeice, 1938*

# [2]

# Man and Zoo

### The staff

It must have been strange being a keeper during the early days of the Society, for there were no precedents to guide the routine work. Over the years there has been a long series of devoted animal keepers, some very distinguished in their own line. The staff of the Society is, however, a many-sided organism, with gardeners, technicians, building craftsmen, office workers and scientists as well as the more familiar keepers with whom the public come into contact.

The first keeper
'The appointment of Mr James Cops, as keeper of the menagerie, at a salary of a guinea per week, was also approved of.'
*Minutes, 24 July 1827*

But not for long ... 'The Committee having reported several acts of misconduct on the part of James Cops the Head Keeper, it was resolved, that he be immediately dismissed upon paying him two months' wages in addition to what are now due, and paying his lodging up to 15 March next.'
*Minutes, 7 February 1828*

Pay rise
'It was reported that Willm Cocksedge who had been hired as a keeper in Sept. last was approved, and his salary was in consequence to be raised from 2/6 to 3/– p. day from 1 January last.
    'It was ordered that a gratuity of £5 be given to W. Cocksedge in consequence of his having some time back been bitten severely by one of the bears.'
*Minutes, 4 February 1829*

An early tragedy
'It being reported that Josiah Graver one of the keeper's helpers had been dangerously injured by the large Arctic bear, it was ordered that every attention be paid to him and his family and that Mr Sabine be requested to attend to the execution of this order. It was also

This Polar Bear was purchased in July 1829 and lived in the Gardens for over fourteen years, despite the Council's instructions after the tragedy in 1830.

ordered that the animal be disposed of.'
*Minutes, 16 June 1830*

'Mr Miller reported that in compliance with the instructions of the last Council, he had provided for the funeral of Josiah Graver, the cost of which £13.10/6 was ordered to be paid, and it was also ordered that the sum of £10 be given to the father of Josiah Graver to reimburse his expenses in travelling from Norfolk to attend his son, and for the purchase of mourning: and it was further ordered that another of his sons should have the offer of the first situation of labourer which might occur in the Garden.'
*Minutes, 7 July 1830*

Discipline
'The Minutes of the Garden Discipline Committee, dated the 7th inst, were read and approved. Williams, Lidd and Hacker, (keepers) were called before the Council—Williams and Lidd were informed

[32]

that the Council, having taken into consideration their long services, and their good conduct, would not enforce their immediately relinquishing their present business—that though the Council refrained from compelling them to make any sacrifice, which, as they represented, would expose them to direct loss of property, they were given to understand that a beer shop is not a concern in which any servant of the Society ought to be engaged; and that it was desired that they should, as soon as possible, quit those which they had taken.'
*Minutes, 9 May 1838*

Keeper of the Chimpanzee. *English Illustrated Magazine,*
*July 1895*

Early catering activities
'It was ordered that the married keepers of the Park shall hereafter
have the privilege in succession according to seniority for their
wives to sell cakes etc. at the two stalls in the Garden, to commence
on 1 January in each year to hold the place for a year: the senior to
have the choice of the place, but on the time coming round again,
the person having had the superior place shall take the inferior.'
*Minutes, 23 June 1832*

'The request of George Jeffery, keeper, for permission to marry,
was granted.'
*Minutes, 15 December 1841*

Tragedy in the Reptile House
'The Secretary reported the death of Edward Horatio Girling, which
had taken place on the morning of the 20th and been occasioned by
the bite of a Cobra (*Naia tripudians*) which he had, while suffering
from the influence of liquor, wilfully and rashly removed from its
case in the Reptile House. The short interval which had elapsed
between the commission of this fatal act, and the meeting of the
Council had not afforded the Secretary sufficient opportunity to
investigate the circumstances thoroughly, but he had ascertained that
the deceased had obtained his last supply of gin at the Albert Public
House in company with six other servants of the Society, at eight
o'clock in the morning.'
*Minutes, 20 October 1852*

Pensions in 1857
'That a pension not exceeding one-third of their actual wages, shall
be given to men who have completed twenty-eight years in the
service of the Society, when they become unfit for work, and that all
men who have been taken on the Establishment subsequently to the
year 1840, shall be immediately required to join some approved
benefit society, with the view of securing provision for themselves in
the event of illness or old age, without charge to the Society.'
*Minutes, 1 April 1857*

Medical attention for the staff
'Resolved ... that the Secretary be authorized to engage Messrs
Lucas and Meehan of No. 8, Taunton Place, Regent's Park, as medical

attendants to the keepers and other servants of the Society employed at the Gardens, with a remuneration of twenty pounds for the twelve months next ensuing from this date.'
*Minutes, 21 July 1858*

Keeper's pay
'In conformity with the report of the same Committee, on considering the reference of the Council regarding the keepers' salaries it was agreed:
    'That the ordinary keepers' monthly salaries be raised from £59.12 per annum to £60 per annum.
    'That after ten years' service their salaries be raised to £66 per annum.
    'That after twenty-five years' service their salaries be raised to £72 per annum.
    'That the Assistant Head Keeper's salary be raised from £86 to £92 per annum.'
*Minutes, 18 January 1865*

A perk for the Assistant Superintendent's wife ... 'Agreed ... That Mrs C. Bartlett be appointed to superintend the Ladies' retiring rooms at the Gardens at a salary of £6 per quarter.'
*Minutes, 18 June 1879*

'That the sum of £5 be given towards the expenses of the annual bean feast of the Society's keepers, workmen and co. employed at the Gardens.'
*Minutes, 21 July 1909*

'That a gratuity of £2 be awarded to A. Macdonald, junior keeper, [who later became the first Head Keeper at Whipsnade Park in 1931] in consideration of his special efforts and success in connection with the rearing of young pheasants and waterfowl.'
*Minutes, 1 February 1911*

First World War
'The Council was of the opinion that members of the staff who were of suitable age and health should be encouraged to join the army for the duration of the war. It was agreed that in such cases the places of the men should be kept open, and that with respect to married

[35]

Three little chimpanzees with their keeper.
*The Sphere, October, 1905*

men the War Office allowance to the wives and families should be made up to full pay, and with respect to unmarried men, two-thirds of the full pay should be reserved for them. It has been found possible to work with a reduced staff during winter, but temporary additional assistance is being provided for spring and summer.'

[The names of thirty-six men, who enlisted in the army, follow: among them keepers, gardeners and a pathologist's attendant.]
*Annual Report, 1914*

Murder for reasons unknown
'In 1928 a sad and inexplicable event took place, unprecedented in
the history of the Society. Sayaid Ali, a Mohammedan mahout, was
killed in the Gardens, and San Dwe, a younger Burmese Karen
Christian, also an elephant keeper, was found guilty of murder,
sentenced to death, but afterwards reprieved and the sentence com-
muted to imprisonment for life. During the end of 1921 and the
following winter, Indiarana, a fine female elephant presented by the
Maharajah of Patiala, which had been accustomed to carry children
in the Gardens, became extremely nervous, and ... it was agreed to
procure the services of a highly skilled Indian mahout, to see if
Indiarana could be brought to reason. Sayaid Ali was selected and
reached the Gardens in July, 1922. He was extremely successful and
very soon the elephant was more docile than she had ever been ...
When the two keepers were together at the Gardens they shared
quarters in the special house that had been built originally for the
white elephant. Sayaid Ali, as the senior and more experienced man,
was given charge of the two refractory elephants, and San Dwe was
given sole care of a very young elephant of which he became fond and
had already begun to teach to do tricks. Both men were well liked
by the other keepers, and, so far as we knew, they were on good terms.
The Mohammedan was a tall and powerful man, but quite good-
natured; the Karen was slightly built, much younger, bright and
lively, and a good musician. Then one night Sayaid Ali was brutally
murdered in his sleep and all the evidence pointed to San Dwe as
the criminal ... The motive was never known ...'
*Centenary History of the Zoological Society,*
*by P. Chalmers Mitchell, 1929*

Long service: nineteenth century
'It was reported that Benjamin Misselbrook having been employed
as a keeper in the month of December, and being approved, was
entitled to the usual salary as keeper, viz. 3/- p. day from April next.'
*Minutes, 18 March 1829*

'An important change in the staff of the Society's Gardens took place
in 1889, owing to the retirement of Mr Benjamin Misselbrook, who
had served the Society as Head Keeper for twenty years, and had
been sixty years and a half altogether in their employment. The Council
thought it right to allow this old and valued officer, who had attained

an advanced age in the Society's service, to retire on full pay, and are certain that they will receive the full approbation of the Fellows in adopting this course.'
*Annual Report, 1889*

'Before leaving the subject of the staff the Council think it right to mention the death of Benjamin Misselbrook, for twenty years Head Keeper in the Gardens, and since 1889 on the pension list. Misselbrook died at the age of eighty-two, after a long and industrious life spent in the Society's service, which he entered as a boy in 1828. Under these circumstances the Council have thought it proper to confer on his widow a pension of £26 a year for the rest of her life.'
*Annual Report, 1893*

And in the twentieth century
'Jack Ward started as a boy of fourteen at the zoo forty-five and a half years ago and became a keeper. Now he is Gardens Executive, responsible for the public gates, fire system, animal rides, weaponry, time-keeping, escape drill and so on.

'When he was five he would sneak in through a hole in the fence. Now his job is to keep out the non-paying public ... "the most re-spectable people try to climb over the roofs to get in free ...

'"I've enjoyed every minute here. Men come here to earn a living but they're totally dedicated.

'"Their work lives on after they've gone. That's a contribution to give any man pride in his job."'
*Daily Mail, London, 7 October 1974*

Mr Ward retired later in 1974 and was appointed M.B.E. in the New Year's Honours, 1975.

In 1973 some fifty-four members of staff had served the Society for twenty-five or more years.

## The Fellows

The members of the Zoological Society are known as Fellows. They have the responsibility of electing the Council and Officers from among their own numbers. Women were admitted as members from the very early days of the Society.

'It was resolved that ladies, proposed by any member of the Council, be admitted as members of the Society on the same terms, and with the same privileges, as gentlemen subscribers.'
*Minutes, 3 April 1827*

'It having been reported to the Council that several Fellows and visitors have insisted on taking their sticks and umbrellas into the Gardens without necessity, and contrary to the regulations made in that case the Superintendent is ordered to obtain the names of such persons and report them to the Council that measures may be adopted to prevent such practice in future.'
*Minutes, 26 April 1832*

Some Fellows infringe the rules
'The Secretary reported that the Earl of Kimberley F.Z.S. had declined to comply with the request of the attendant not to smoke on the lawn of the Society's Gardens on Sunday the 26th ult. whereupon it was agreed that a letter be addressed to Lord Kimberley explaining the circumstances under which the regulation against smoking had been made, and requesting him not to infringe it in future.'
*Minutes, 5 June 1867*

Visits 'behind the scenes' are not always welcome. 'The statistics as to breeding are also not wholly satisfactory as an indication of the general state of health of the animals, for the obvious reason that a collection intended primarily for exhibition requires different arrangements from one suitable for breeding. An instructive example is the breeding of lions. For the first time for over a quarter of a century the Society bred and reared two litters of lions. The success was due to several reasons. Sir Edward Northey had presented two very fine young males which were mated with two lionesses already in the collection. Very special care was given by the new Curator of Mammals to the housing and feeding of the mothers, both before and after birth.

But probably the most important factor was securing absolute privacy for the mother and cubs for many weeks, which could be done only by forbidding the keepers to take Fellows or visitors "behind the scenes"—a step which caused many protests.'
*Annual Report, 1923*

Looking for Fellows
'WHAT BOYS CANNOT SEE AT THE ZOO, fruitless search for a Fellow. Intelligence, aged nine, at the Zoo yesterday, somewhat bored with feeding the lions and riding camels: "Take me to the place where they keep the Fellows, father."

' "Hush, my son," returned the fond parent. "They do not keep the Fellows; the Fellows keep the Zoo. Besides, you cannot see them. They only come on Sunday, when the likes of us are not admitted. I will take you instead to see the wild asses."

'The boy was obviously disappointed. He pondered the information for some time until he noticed the man who picks up waste paper. "Oh, father," cried he, "is not that a Fellow?" The parent was a little angered. "How often," he retorted, "have I told you to be respectful to our ancient institutions? That good man is a fellow in the abstract, but not a Fellow with a capital F. The Fellows are not ordinary men. They do not mix with the common people on a Bank Holiday, when the admission is sixpence. You see that nice clean building over there, with the beautiful garden and the pretty waitresses. That is where the Fellows go on Sunday to take their tea—and other refreshments."

'Nine years old, still persistent, returned to the charge. "Could I not even see a cinematograph picture of a Fellow?" he asked.

'Father, by now rather tired: "No, you cannot. Motion pictures are not permitted to be taken within the Zoo. If you are a good boy, and stop asking questions, I will shortly take you to the waxworks, and show you the Chamber of Horrors."

'"Shall I see a Fellow there, father?" pleaded the boy.'
*Daily Express, 6 April 1920*

The Fellows' privileges go on
'WHOSE ZOO? Tomorrow is the Day of Rest. Rest, that is, for those who have tasks and duties. For the idlers it is one more day of boredom. It would be a fine day for taking the children to the Zoo to see the polar bears diving into the water and to ride on the elephant.

Making up for the 'Days of Rest' that they were unable to spend
at the Zoo, hundreds of families flocked to the Gardens on
August Bank Holiday 1922 when the gates were opened
to the public, and not just idle Fellows!

On the Day of Rest, however, the Zoo is closed to the public. It is
open for the Fellows of the Royal Zoological Society. There is no
particular distinction about them except that they pay a subscription
of three pounds a year.'
*The Daily Express, 27 May 1933*

But the war brings changes
'In 1847 there was never any question of the public being admitted
for payment on Sunday, for the simple reason that, until 1932, when
the Sunday Entertainments Act was passed, such a step would have
been illegal. In 1940, the Council realized that the Society's revenues
were likely to be very adversely affected by the war, and in consequence decided to open the Gardens to the public on Sundays

after 1 p.m., and to service personnel and their friends throughout the day. When hostilities ended in 1945, the ruling was altered, and the time of opening was delayed until 2.30 p.m. This later opening did not prevent Sundays from being the day on which the public made proportionally their greatest contribution to the Society's revenues.'
*Annual Report, 1957*

Corresponding members
These are members living overseas who give a great deal of help in advancing the Society's aims. Many Corresponding Members (C.M.Z.S.) played an important part in the Society's work, particularly in the nineteenth century. They have provided large numbers of animals for the Zoo, and still continue to do so.

One of the first circular letters to Corresponding Members has been preserved:

'Zoological Society, 33, Bruton Street, 1827.

'Sir, I take the liberty, ... of sending to you the last report of the Zoological Society.

'It is possible that, in the course of your residence at ... opportunities of promoting our views and objects may occur to you, and that you may be able to send to us occasionally, and at a very inconsiderable expense, specimens of subjects in Zoology of much curiosity and interest.

'Living specimens of all rare animals, and particularly of such as may possibly be domesticated and become useful here, will be much valued by us; and above all varieties of the deer kind, and of gallinaceous birds; but beyond this preserved insects, reptiles, birds, mammalia, fishes, eggs, and shells will be gratefully received.

'And I may mention that where a more scientific method does not occur, the promiscuous immersion of any number of subjects in a tub of strong brine (feathers, bodies, and all) will be sufficient for preservation, not quite effectual perhaps for the skins of all instances, but perfectly so for purposes of dissection and comparative anatomy.'

'Read a letter, dated Falmouth 20 July from Lieut C. Smith, of H.M. brig *Star*, Corresponding Member, announcing his arrival from Trinidad with a pair of agoutis for the Society's menagerie, and some preserved specimens for the Museum. It was ordered that the thanks

of the Society be returned to Lieut Smith for these donations.'
*Minutes, 29 July 1840*

Colonel Samuel Richard Tickell, C.M.Z.S., first went to India in
1828 as an officer in the Bengal Army of the Honourable East India
Company. His manuscripts on the birds, mammals, reptiles and fishes
of Bengal and Burma are still in the Library of the Zoological Society.

'The number of Corresponding Members at present on the lists of
the Society amounts to 141; and the Council are happy to announce
that the zeal of this useful class of our Associates for the advancement
of the Society continues to be manifested with unabated ardour, as
is proved by the numerous donations both to the menagerie and
Museum ... Among those elected during the past year, the Council
have a peculiar satisfaction in referring to the name of Sir Jamsetgee
Jejubhoy of Bombay, a gentleman already honourably known for the
munificent patronage which he extends to the charitable and scientific
institutions of his native country, and who has acquired the well-
merited approbation of his sovereign in the first knighthood ever
conferred on a native of British India. Conjointly with his friend
A.N.Shade, Esq. of the Honourable Company's Civil Service at
Dharwar, also an active and zealous Corresponding Member, to
whom the Council are under many obligations, Sir Jamsetgee Jejubhoy
has already, with his customary generosity, transmitted, at his own
cost, a number of valuable animals to the Society's menagerie, some
of which have already arrived, and others are shortly expected.'
*Annual Report, 1842*

'The most important event connected with the Society's menagerie
that has occurred since the last anniversary has been the successful
result of Mr Thompson's mission to India ...
  'Several of the Society's Corresponding Members in India ...
having announced that they had collections waiting for transmission
to the Society, amongst which were a pair of young rhinoceroses, and
other valuable animals, the Council determined on sending out to
Calcutta, to receive and bring back those proffered donations, Mr
James Thompson, the Society's Head Keeper, who had previously
made the same journey with such signal success on the occasion of
the introduction of the Himalayan Pheasants in 1858. They also
gladly embraced the opportunity of sending out to the Babu Rajendra

23

*Naja lutescens?*

(Laurenti.)

Tenasserim variety?

A page on the Indian Cobra from the manuscript that Colonel
Tickell presented to the Society in 1874

Mullick a selection of living animals likely to be acceptable to that gentleman, as some return for the many valuable donations that he has from time to time made to the Society's menagerie ... Mr Thompson left Calcutta on his return voyage in the *Hydaspes* on 5 April, and arrived in the Thames on 28 July, bringing with him the following fine series of animals, which had been brought together for the Society at Calcutta by the exertions of their Corresponding Members, the Babu Rajendra Mullick of Calcutta, Mr A. Grote of Alipore, Dr John Squire, and Mr Wm Dunn of Akyab: 2 Rhinoceroses, 2 Black Cuckoos, 2 Rose-coloured Pastors, 1 Rhinoceros Hornbill, 2 Concave Hornbills, 3 Green-necked Peafowl, 3 Lineated Pheasants, 2 Rufous-tailed Pheasants, 1 Peacock Pheasant, 2 Indian Tantali, 2 Indian Jabirus, 2 Sarus Cranes, 2 Land Tortoises.'
*Annual Report, 1864*

'CORRESPONDING MEMBERS. Twenty-seven Corresponding Members, most of whom were subjects of countries now at war with Great Britain, were removed from the List under By-law Chap. VI., Sect. iv.' [At the same time fourteen distinguished zoologists from thirteen different countries were elected Corresponding Members.]
*Annual Report, 1916*

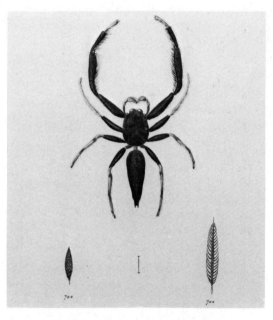

A tropical spider painted in Penang, Malaya on 25
September 1842 by Theodore Edward Cantor, M.D.,
Bengal Medical Service, Calcutta,
a Corresponding Member

## Royal visitors and patrons

Throughout its history the Zoological Society of London has enjoyed the interest and patronage of the Royal Family, from the time of King George IV up to the present day.

His Royal Highness Prince Philip, Duke of Edinburgh, is now the President of the Society.

Princess Victoria visits the Zoo
'Today R. and I set off to the Zoological Gardens. We had only been there a few minutes when the Duchess of Kent and the Princess Victoria came in. The gentleman who gave his arm to the Princess was an elder brother of the King of the Netherlands and brother to the Duchess of Kent. His eldest son supported his aunt. The Duchess looked very well, and as amiable as usual. She had on an exquisite satin dress, a very dark ground thickly strewed with gorgeous flowers, and a canary-coloured bonnet with roses. The Princess had on a delicate sort of salmon-coloured checked silk, with a cape, and a sky-blue satin bonnet. She is very fair, and looks clever and unaffected. They walked all over the gardens, Mr Bennett doing the honours in a very pleasing manner. I was thankful to see the other visitors did not press the royal party, and it was very pleasant to see the good feeling which welcomed them on every side. They took great pains to visit and see everything worth seeing, and seemed to greatly enjoy the actions of the seal diving for fish.'
*Mrs Owen's diary, 20 March 1836, from The Life of Richard Owen, by Richard Owen, 1894*

And, as Queen Victoria, becomes Patroness
'A letter was read from the President in answer to the one addressed to his Lordship by desire of the Council at the last meeting, as was also a letter, which accompanied it, from Lord Melbourne, stating, that Her Majesty had been graciously pleased to signify her consent to become the Patroness of the Society.'
*Minutes, 16 August 1837*

Queen Victoria presents a tigress
'Read a letter from Colonel Bowles enclosing one from Baron Montcorvo the Portuguese Minister which accompanied a present of a tigress from Her Most Faithful Majesty to Her Most Gracious Majesty the Queen, and announcing that "The Queen is graciously

The first Alpaca was presented by King William IV to the Society on 26 August 1830. This engraving of the same year was based on a drawing by W. Panormo

pleased to offer the said beautiful tigress to the Zoological Society."

'Ordered, that Colonel Bowles be requested to lay before Her Majesty the special thanks of the Society for this gracious mark of Her Majesty's royal favour.'
*Minutes, 2 July 1845*

The Prince Consort becomes President
'On Friday he received a further letter from Colonel Grey stating, that H.R.H. was willing to accept of the office of President ...

'Upon which it was resolved unanimously: That the Council learn with great satisfaction that H.R.H. Prince Albert has been pleased to accede to their request that he would accept the office of President of the Society.

'Resolved also: That as the Charter directs that the President must be selected from among the Fellows of the Society, the Council immediately admit H.R.H. a Fellow ...

[47]

'The Council then proceeded to the election of a President, in pursuance of the provisions of the Charter, in the room of the late Earl of Derby, when H.R.H. Prince Albert was unanimously elected.'
*Minutes, 21 July 1851*

'It was then resolved that the Secretary be directed to ascertain if possible whether His Royal Highness the President would be disposed to receive into the royal domains a male and two female elands with the prospect of their breeding and becoming domesticated in this country, subject to the Society having a desirable offer for their sale, which the state of the funds of the Society make necessary if possible.'
*Minutes, 16 May 1855*

Death of the Prince Consort
(President of the Society, 1851–61)
'The Secretary announced the death of His Royal Highness the Prince Consort, President of the Society, whereupon it was unanimously resolved:
'That the Council cannot allow this, their first meeting since the death of their lamented President, to pass over without desiring to record on their Minutes their deep sense of the great loss the Society has thereby sustained.'
*Minutes, 18 December 1861*

Queen Victoria visits the Zoological Gardens
'COURT CIRCULAR. Buckingham Palace, 4 March. The Queen, accompanied by Princess Beatrice, drove to Regent's Park this morning, attended by Lady Waterpark and the Hon. Caroline Cavendish, and visited the Zoological Gardens. The equerries-in-waiting were in attendance on horseback.'
*The Times, 5 March 1869*

The Prince of Wales presents an alligator
'That the special thanks of the Society be offered to H.R.H. the Prince of Wales for his acceptable present of an alligator.'
*Minutes, 18 January 1871*

The Prince of Wales' Indian Collection
'The most noticeable event connected with the menagerie in 1876

# Zoological Gardens,
## REGENT'S PARK.

## Reception, June 16th, 1887.

### Patroness.
HER MAJESTY QUEEN VICTORIA.

### Vice * Patron.
HIS ROYAL HIGHNESS THE PRINCE OF WALES, K.G.

### President.
PROFESSOR FLOWER, LL.D., V.P.R.S.

### Secretary.
PHILIP LUTLEY SCLATER, Esq., M.A., Ph.D., F.R.S.

### Refreshment Tent.

TEA, COFFEE, BREAD AND BUTTER, CAKE,
FRENCH PASTRY, BISCUITS, &c.
STRAWBERRY, VANILLA, CREAM, AND
LEMON WATER ICES.
GRAPES, STRAWBERRIES & CREAM.

FK. TROTMAN & SONS, Purveyors.

A party was held on the lawns of the Gardens to celebrate
Queen Victoria's Golden Jubilee in 1887

was the deposit in the Gardens of the fine collection of Indian animals belonging to the Prince of Wales.

'I. MAMMALS. 2 Green Monkeys, 2 Rhesus Monkeys, 5 Tigers, 7 Leopards, 1 Cheetah, 1 Viverrine Cat, 1 Indian Civet, 4 Tailless Dogs, 3 Tibetan Mastiffs, 2 White Dogs, 2 Indian Wild Dogs, 1 Himalayan Bear, 1 Sloth Bear, 4 Indian Elephants, 6 Domestic Sheep, 2 Thar Goats, 4 Shawl-goats, 8 Indian Antelopes, 2 Zebus, 2 Spotted Porcine Deer, 3 Axis Deer, 2 Musk Deer. II. BIRDS. 1 Grey-winged Blackbird, 2 Wedge-tailed Pigeons, 5 Domestic Pigeons, 8 Surat Doves, 1 Black Francolin, 2 Hill-Francolins, 4 Chukar Partridges, 15 Impeyan Pheasants, 21 Cheer Pheasants, 2 Pucras Pheasants, 4 White-crested Kaleeges, 3 Bankiva Jungle Fowl, 10 Horned Tragopans, 5 Indian Peafowl, 3 Ostriches.

'The Collection arrived in May, 1876, in excellent order, under the charge of our Assistant Superintendent (Mr Clarence Bartlett), who in 1875 had received special leave of absence from the Council, for the purpose of accompanying the Prince of Wales during his Indian tour as Zoological Collector. The Collection remained, it is needless to say, a source of very great attraction to the Fellows of the Society and to the visitors to the Gardens throughout the summer, and tended very materially ... to increase the Garden's receipts.'
*Annual Report, 1876*

The Nepal Collection
'There was read a letter addressed to the President of the Society from Sir Walter Lawrence in which it was stated that the Nepal Government had offered a collection of Nepalese animals to the Prince of Wales, and that the Prince of Wales had offered them to the Society on the condition that he should not be called upon to pay the cost of bringing the collection to England. The President having stated that he was ready to defray this expense himself.

'Resolved: That the collection of Nepalese animals be accepted, and that a letter of thanks to H.R.H. the Prince of Wales be prepared.

'Resolved: That the best thanks of the Council be given to His Grace the Duke of Bedford, K.G., President of the Society, for his generous promise to defray the cost of transport to England of a collection of animals presented to the Prince of Wales by the Government of Nepal, and by the Prince to the Zoological Society.

'It was agreed that Arthur Thomson, Assistant Superintendent at the Gardens, and John Shelley, 2nd class keeper, should be sent to

Calcutta to return with the collection, that the collection should be sent down from Nepal to the Calcutta Gardens, and there be packed for shipment to London.'
*Minutes, 21 February 1906*

The death of King Edward VII, 1910
'THE PATRON OF THE SOCIETY. In the course of the year, the Society has had to share in the grief of the whole nation at the death of His late Most Gracious Majesty King Edward VII.

'In 1876 His Royal Highness deposited in the Society's Gardens the collection of animals made on his Indian tour. The number of visitors to the Gardens in that year rose from nearly 700,000 to over 900,000, and the increased receipts made possible a number of permanent improvements.'
*Annual Report, 1910*

King George V becomes Patron
'In June, 1910, the Council had the great pleasure of announcing to the Fellows that the King had been graciously pleased to become Patron of the Society in succession to His late Majesty King Edward. Thus the long and fortunate association between the Society and the Royal House remains unbroken. In 1829 King George IV granted to the Society a Royal Charter; in 1830 King William IV became Patron and presented to the Society all the animals belonging to the Royal

King George V and Queen Mary visit the new Aquarium in
April 1924

Menagerie in Windsor Park; in 1837 Queen Victoria became Patroness of the Society. The Prince Consort was our President from 1851 until 1861; King Edward became Vice-Patron in 1864 and Patron in 1901.

'His Majesty King George V became a Fellow of the Society in 1894 and Vice-Patron in 1901; in 1906 he deposited with the Society the very interesting set of animals which had been presented to him during his official tour in India as Prince of Wales. His Majesty has graciously consented to deposit with the Society a collection of African animals, chiefly presented by various public and private donors in South Africa. The collection is expected to arrive in England in May and to be exhibited as the King's African Collection throughout the summer.'
*Annual Report, 1910*

Princess Elizabeth at Whipsnade
'PRINCESS REFUSES ROSE. Princess Elizabeth, who has just celebrated her eighth birthday, was taken by the King and Queen to Whipsnade Zoo yesterday.

'While tea was being served Sir Peter Chalmers Mitchell offered

A royal visit to Regent's Park in 1967

her one of the red roses with which the table was decorated. She caused amusement by refusing it, saying "No, I'm York." '
*Daily Herald, 24 April 1934*

H.R.H. Prince Philip becomes President
'The Society was deeply honoured by the gracious acceptance of the Presidency by His Royal Highness, The Prince Philip, Duke of Edinburgh, who was elected at the Anniversary Meeting on the 29 April ...

'In accepting office, the new President sent the following message:

'"I should like you to tell the Council of the Zoological Society, and the Annual General Meeting of the Society on 29 April, that I greatly appreciate the honour of becoming the President of the Society. During my term of office I shall do my best to further the Society's purposes, and the Society can count on my help in the task of relandscaping and rebuilding the Regent's Park Gardens. I am delighted that the Society's new plans have got off to such a splendid start."'
*Annual Report, 1960*

## The other visitors

In the early days only Fellows or those with a Fellow's authority were allowed into the Zoological Gardens, but there were some exceptions.

Local children were admitted, but only early in the morning. 'The Secretary ... also reported that having been applied to by the church-wardens of St Pancras Parish, for permission that the children of the parish should visit the Gardens, he had complied with their request, appointing an early hour of the day for their visit.'
*Minutes, 7 October 1829*

Sabbath and Zoo
'TO THE EDITOR OF THE TIMES. Sir, In riding round the Regent's Park yesterday, Sunday afternoon, I observed a number of carriages at the entrance of the Zoological Gardens, and several persons of both sexes entering the gardens.

'Through the medium of your widely circulated journal, I beg to inquire of some of the governors, whether it is not an infringement of the Sabbath, in thus making the animals confined in the Gardens objects of public amusement, and whether six days in the week are not sufficient for such an amusement.

'I am, Sir, yours, &c. Scrutator.'
Queen Square, Monday morning
*The Times, 19 October 1830*

'TO THE EDITOR OF THE TIMES. Sir, In answer to Scrutator's letter, in this day's *Times*, allow me, through the same medium, to inform him, that the Zoological Gardens are not open to the public generally, on Sundays, but only to the Fellows of the Society, who are permitted to enter with two friends, and which is a great convenience to many of them, who might otherwise be prevented from visiting the Gardens.

'As to its being an infringement of the sabbath, Query, Is not Scrutator's riding round the Park on that day, equally so? or the public walking in Kensington Gardens, in which there are as many keepers required as in the Zoological Gardens?

'I am, Sir, your obedient servant, F.Z.S.'
*The Times, 20 October 1830*

## ALL THE DIFFERENCE.

" MAMMA, DEAR, MRS. ROBINSON HAS WRITTEN TO ASK IF I WILL GO WITH
HER TO THE "ZOO" NEXT SUNDAY. I *SHOULD* SO LIKE TO!"

" *WHAT*, MY DEAR! ON *SUNDAY!* NEVER!"

"WHY, BUT WE GO TO THE KENSINGTON GARDENS!"

" I DISAPPROVE OF LOOKING AT BEASTS ON SUNDAY!"

" BUT THE PEOPLE LOOK AT EACH OTHER, MAMMA; NOT AT THE BEASTS.'

" IF YOU ARE *SURE* OF THAT, MY DEAR, YOU MAY ACCEPT MRS. ROBINSON'S
INVITATION."

*Punch, July, 1866*

Catering for the visitors
'A Report was read from the Committee appointed on the 9th inst
to consider the subject of allowing ices, etc. to be sold at the Gardens,
wherein it was recommended that permission be granted for the sale
of ices and confectionery of a superior description at the Gardens,
and that tenders be applied for from the more respectable con-
fectioners for such purpose. It was moved and carried that this
recommendation be adopted.'
*Minutes, 16 July 1834*

[55]

Visitors coming by train
'Resolved also that the Secretary be authorized to make such arrangements as he may judge expedient, for the admission of passengers by railway excursion trains to the Gardens.'
*Minutes, 16 October 1850*

'Read a Report from the Secretary which stated that complaints had been made in the public prints, as well as to himself privately of the want of a supply of water for drinking, by visitors to the Gardens.

'Upon which it was ordered that measures should be taken for giving convenience to the visitors in respect of this want.'
*Minutes, 6 July 1853*

'Read a Report from the Secretary, in which he stated that he had received offers in writing from Mr Miller the present tenant, and from Mr Huson of Albany Street to rent the Refreshment Rooms at the Gardens for twelve months from 1 April 1857 to 31 March 1858, for the sum of £400.

'It was resolved that the offer of Mr Miller be accepted, provided that he consent to pay the whole rent of £400 in advance without deduction, and undertake to execute such an agreement as may be approved by the Council, to ensure proper service to the visitors.'
*Minutes, 18 March 1857*

Visitors to the Den of Bears

'The following Motion of which Dr Percy had given notice at the last meeting, was then discussed and being seconded by Mr I.B. Beresford Hope, M.P., was put and carried, namely:

'That the Tenant of the Refreshment Room shall in future be permitted to supply refreshment on Sunday between the hours of 2 p.m. and 7 p.m.'
*Minutes, 17 June 1857*

### Wrong gear

'Read letters from Messrs Mivart & Ackerley respecting the gate-keepers' refusal to admit certain persons to whom they had given admissions to the Gardens on the ground of their being badly dressed.'
*Minutes, 21 July 1858*

### Worth a try

'Read a letter from Messrs Aldridge, Bromley, & Co. of Bedford Row, stating that Mr Edwin John Abraham of the Record Office Chancery Lane had been knocked down and injured by the little African elephant in the Society's Gardens on the 4th inst and requesting compensation for him.

'The Secretary reported that he had made strict enquiry into the circumstances, and that two keepers, and a third witness, who was near, all deposed that the elephant had not touched Mr Abraham, on the occasion in question, and that he had accordingly replied to Messrs Aldridge & Co. declining to give any compensation.

'This was approved of.'
*Minutes, 17 October 1866*

'SATURDAY AFTERNOON AT THE ZOOLOGICAL GARDENS. I like the Zoological Gardens; there is so much to be seen and heard that is congenial to the kindlier feelings of man, and it shows a high state of civilization when a great and overcrowded city devotes part of its energies and space to the preservation and kindly treatment of animals, which the savage looks upon as things made solely and on purpose to be hunted and destroyed. More especially are the Regent's Park gardens delightful on a Saturday afternoon in the summer time ...

'A famous place for children this is, and much they enjoy their usual Saturday half holiday in these gardens. A little amusing excitement does children much good, particularly if it induces them to run about in the open air; for fresh air is as necessary to their growth

The 'little fair-haired Saxon ... pulling at his father's hand.'
*The Leisure Hour, September, 1859*

as water is to young plants. It is curious also to remark the disposition of these little ones. Here comes a little fair-haired Saxon, clad in the garb of a Scotchman; his little kilt, sporran, and dirk make him strut along quite proud of his sturdy sunburnt limbs, and he is perpetually pulling at his father's hand. "Oh! do come here Papa; look at the bear. Oh! I think I should like to climb the pole like that;" a few minutes afterwards: "Oh! Papa, I have not seen the monkeys; let's go and see the monkeys." But before he gets to the Monkey House,

the seal, splashing in the water, attracts his attention, and he runs round and round the seal's enclosure, watching him dive and come up again, as though he was playing a merry game of hide-and-seek.'
*The Leisure Hour, September 1859*

The Zoo continues to attract people of all classes
'The number of visitors in 1866 was 527,349, against 525,176 in 1865. Of these 107,417 paid one shilling each for admission, while 282,315 paid only sixpence, showing that the Zoological Society, like the railways, draws its chief revenue from the working classes. Judging, however, from the state of the Broad Walk on Sunday afternoons, and the unfailing supply of candidates for the Fellowship the Gardens appear to be not less popular among the more exclusive ranks of Society.'
*Saturday Revue, May 1867*

But no cheap rate on Saturdays
'A letter was read from C.Hill, Esq. Secretary of the Working Men's Lord's Day Rest Associations, suggesting the desirability of opening the Society's Gardens on Saturday afternoons to the working classes at sixpence each—to which it was agreed to reply that this experiment had already been tried, and had not proved successful.'
*Minutes, 15 December 1869*

'The Zoological Gardens are simply the most popular exhibition in London. We all go to the British Museum for instruction's sake; but we visit the Zoological Gardens for amusement as well as for instruction. The South Kensington and the Tower have their partisans; but then we are not all artists or "country cousins" ...'
*Daily Telegraph, 4 January 1870*

Unwelcome visitors
'Though bears are very good climbers, yet it is a mercy they cannot jump, or otherwise they would have long ago jumped out of the bear-pit from the top of their pole. Some years back a young man, on a sixpenny day, had an adventure with the bear. I suppose the heat of the weather (or other disturbing causes) made him drop his best holiday hat right into the bear-pit. The stupid fellow at once got down into the bear-pit, alighting on the top of a big bear who was coiled up sleeping in the sun. The bear got up, and taking the man by the

[59]

'Saturday afternoon is essentially a lounging time; music and zoology on that day join hand to hand; the senses of sight and hearing are both gratified, all at the cost of one shilling. Reader, whether you are fond of music or natural history, or maybe both, we hope to meet you next Saturday at the Zoological Gardens at four o'clock, and you will see for yourself what we have imperfectly endeavoured to describe.'

*The Leisure Hour, September, 1859*

shoulders, began waltzing round with him. Luckily the man kept his feet, and nothing worse happened, as the keeper drove off the bear, and let the man out at the side door. He forgot, however, to take his hat with him, and left it in the cage; the bears, of course, tore it up. The cool impertinence of this man was greatly to be wondered at, as next day he actually sent in a bill to the Society for a new hat.

'Ladies must take notice that Mr Bartlett is not responsible for bonnets or feathers stolen by the monkeys. He was once summoned by an old woman for a bonnet. The old woman produced a shabby old bonnet in court which she valued at an exorbitant price. Mr

Bartlett, on the other side, produced the notice-board from the Monkey House warning visitors against the peculating propensities of the monkeys. The old woman lost her case.'
*Life of Frank Buckland, by G.C.Bompas, 1885*

Another unwelcome visitor
'At Marylebone yesterday, Walter Hamilton Goodfellow, 27, described as a gentleman, living at Ladbroke Gardens, Kensington, was charged on remand with stealing a bell bird, valued at £10, the property of the Zoological Society ... It was shown that on Friday last the prisoner visited the Gardens at Regent's Park, and was seen hurrying out of the Birds' House. The keeper suspected that something was wrong, especially as the birds were making a great noise, and on looking round found that the cage containing the bell bird had been removed, and the bird extracted from it. While the search was going on the prisoner was noticed by another keeper to go into the lavatory and come out again immediately. He was stopped as he was going through the grounds, and when questioned about the bird he pretended that he knew nothing about it. A feather of the bird was, however, on the outside of his coat, and there were others inside his coat pocket. He was detained, and afterwards Mr Bartlett, the Superintendent of the Gardens, saw the prisoner, who then offered to give £20 if he was permitted to go. This was refused, and he was given into custody. The bird was found dead ... Mr Cooke said that he failed to understand how the prisoner came to behave in such an extraordinary manner ... It was abominable conduct to go into these Gardens, which were admirably kept up and looked after, and take a bird because the keeper, who could not be at the heels of every visitor, happened to be out of sight. He fined the prisoner £5, and ordered him to pay £10, the value of the bird. The money was immediately paid.'
*The Times, 1 August 1888*

The Coronation of King Edward VII
'That the request of the Colonial Troops Entertainment Committee that a limited number of passes might be given for the use of the Indian and Colonial Troops to be in this country on the occasion of the King's Coronation be granted, such passes not to be available on Saturdays, Sundays, or Mondays.'
*Minutes, 7 May 1902*

[61]

Courting Europe
'A letter having been read from Mr J. Cathcart Wason, M.P., it was agreed to grant him 60 red tickets available on Sunday for the use of a party of French visitors in connection with L'Entente Cordiale League.'
*Minutes, 17 May 1905*

The Great War
'TEMPORARY ARRANGEMENTS FOR ADMISSION TO THE GAR-DENS. The Council has made the following arrangements, to hold good during the War, or until further notice. 1 The families of Soldiers and Sailors on Active Service will be admitted free, by the time-keepers' gate, on production of the identity certificate in the case of the Regular and Territorial Forces, and of the allotment certificate in the case of naval ratings. 2 Wounded soldiers or sailors will be admitted free on Sundays, on application at the office. 3 Saturdays as well as Mondays will be sixpenny days. 4 Tickets for British and Colonial troops or sailors, and for Belgian refugees may be purchased at the office, at the rate of 3d. each for Mondays and Saturdays, and 6d. each for other weekdays.'
*Annual Report, 1914*

A new idea
'LATE NIGHTS AT THE ZOO. New decision by council. Nocturnal sights. (By our Zoo Correspondent.) The desire often expressed in many quarters that we should introduce more of the Continental ways of life is steadily taking form, and the Zoo is by no means behind the movement.

'The Zoological Society's Council has arranged that throughout the coming summer season the Gardens will be open till 11 p.m. on Saturdays as well as Thursdays, and we shall be able to recall plea-surable evenings at Berlin, Vienna, Antwerp, and elsewhere. It will be possible to dine beneath the trees with band accompaniment, and after the meal to wander away amongst the many paths and listen to such other music that can be heard only in the Zoo—and at night.

'Only on a summer evening can the visitor realize the wealth of animal life that breakfasts at nightfall and dines at dawn. The Rodent House, in which the majority of the nocturnal boarders are housed, will be illuminated by artificial moonlight, which will satisfy the demands of the exhibits and enable the visitor to view shy denizens of desert and jungle disporting themselves.

'In this house on Thursday and Saturday nights one will always find "At Home" the huge Indian fruit bats, porcupine ant-eaters, jerboas, douracoulis, bushbabies, and a dozen other animals that are normally familiar only to the night-watchman.'
*The Observer, 5 March 1933*

But some Fellows object
'CRITICISM OF ZOO CHANGES. First Elements of Unrest. Various changes at the Zoo were criticized at the annual meeting of the Zoological Society at Regent's Park yesterday.

'Lady Portsea said the study of animal life must be carried out in a quiet way. For that reason she was rather against the opening of the Gardens at night and the introduction of the children's playground, both of which seemed to introduce the first elements of unrest.

'Lady Portsea also criticized the increase in electric lighting and referred to a rumour she had heard that a swimming bath was to be built in the Gardens. She hoped that the Council, in agreeing to those changes, would not alter the character of the Gardens.

'Sir Arthur Smith Woodward, who presided, said that open evenings at the Zoo were very popular last year, over 64,000 visitors being admitted. Consequently the Gardens would be open on two evenings each week this summer, Wednesdays and Thursdays, from 3 June to 10 September.'
*The Times, 30 April 1936*

At Whipsnade some visitors need controlling
'WHIPSNADE OSTRICH'S FEATHERS PLUCKED, WOMAN FINED. Lily Greatbatch, of Curdworth Green Cottage, Curdworth, near Birmingham, who was one of a party of visitors to Whipsnade, was yesterday fined £1 and ordered to pay 10s. costs at Leighton Buzzard for interfering with an ostrich by pulling out its feathers.

'Mr Lathom, prosecuting for the Zoological Society, said that Greatbatch was with a party and was seen to put her arm through the railing and pull a feather from an ostrich's wing.

'It was a stupid and wanton act of folly, he continued, and what was worse instead of anyone protesting everyone seemed to enjoy it as a joke. If her example had been followed several feathers would have been pulled out of the ostrich and the bird might have been left naked.

[63]

'A park police officer said that there were fifteen to twenty people at the enclosure. Greatbatch plucked a feather about eight inches long and gave it to a man. All the party laughed. She then put her arm through the enclosure again and pulled out another feather.

'A letter was read from Greatbatch in which she stated that she was sorry she committed the offence, but did not realize she was breaking the law. Now she realized that it was wrong and silly.

'Dr Square, the presiding magistrate, said that if this sort of thing continued the Zoo might have to be shut up.'
*Morning Post, 29 August 1935*

John Gould, F.R.S.

## Some personalities

The Zoological Society has attracted many interesting personalities to its staff and to its Fellowship who have made valuable contributions to its work.

### John Gould

In 1827 John Gould was appointed taxidermist for the Museum of the Zoological Society of London, then in Bruton Street. He later left this employment and started to produce his famous folio volumes on birds, illustrated by beautifully prepared coloured plates. Many of these were the work of his wife, Mary, whom he married in 1829, and of Edward Lear. In all, Gould produced forty-one folio volumes, illustrated by 2,999 plates.

In 1851, the year of the Great Exhibition, he exhibited a collection of preserved humming birds in a building that was later converted into the present Parrot House.

Queen Victoria visited this exhibition on 10 June 1857, an event recorded by *The Times* on the following day: 'Her Majesty occupied a considerable period of her visit in inspecting the celebrated collection of humming birds which has been placed in the Garden by Mr Gould. The admirable manner in which this beautiful group is illustrated, and the extreme rarity of several of the species, have rendered the building in which they are contained a most important addition to the previous attractions of the establishment, and supplied in the only possible manner a great desideratum in the ornithological part of the Society's collection. The visitors who have repaired to the Gardens for the purpose of examining the humming birds include the most distinguished names in science and in art, as well as in rank, and they have universally expressed their surprise and admiration at the unexpected extent of the species, the peculiar forms of their plumage, and the intense brilliancy of colour for which they are remarkable above every other part of the animal kingdom.'
*The Times, 11 June 1857*

### Bartlett: The great Victorian Superintendent

A.D.Bartlett (1812–97) was appointed Superintendent of the Zoological Gardens in July 1859, at a salary of two hundred pounds per annum, and a house, rent free. He was directly responsible for the management of the Gardens to the Secretary and Council of the Zoological Society.

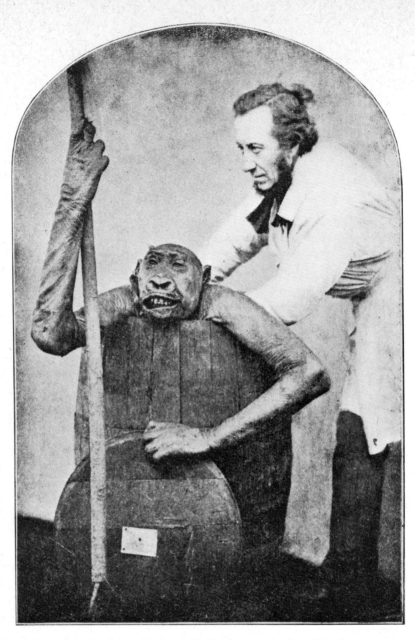

Portrait of A.D. Bartlett with his first preserved gorilla, taken
by Peter Ashton in 1858

Bartlett was the son of a barber in the Strand. 'My origin is a
very humble one. My father (John Bartlett) was apprenticed to and,
after serving his apprenticeship, employed by the father of one of
the greatest of English painters, whose name was Turner. But my

father, as a tonsorial artist, used the brush upon living portraits which are no more, while young Turner's brush was wielded in oil-colour on canvas to represent living portraits, and consequently the wonderful productions of his brush are to this day preserved.

'I had, however, one opportunity which laid the foundation of, and the stepping-stone to, my insatiable love for animals. Mr Turner lived in Exeter Street, Strand, and the wonderful collection of wild beasts was then at Exeter 'Change. It was here that I was, during my infancy, introduced to wild animals. Mr Cross, the proprietor, being a great friend of my father, allowed me a free entrée to that very remarkable and interesting menagerie. In consequence of my early introduction to wild animals, almost before I could walk, I being allowed to crawl about in the beast-room of that menagerie, playing with young lions and other animals that were not likely to harm me, I have not the remotest recollection of seeing for the first time lions, tigers, elephants, or any other wild beasts, simply because I was almost from my birth among them. Since then I have had the good fortune to have the management of the extensive collection of the Zoological Society, and the familiarity with wild beasts in my infancy has been of invaluable service to me.

'During the early period of my life, Mr Cross, noticing how fond I was of living birds and other animals, kindly offered me the dead bodies of some of the birds which I was so fond of feeding. This led me to endeavour to save their beautiful feathers and skins from decay. I was not long in being able to take off and prepare their skins so as to preserve them for future use. The result of this was that I became a successful taxidermist.

'It was from about 1820 to 1826 that I was allowed to walk about the beast-room, as it was then called, at Exeter 'Change. My next seven or eight years were less agreeable, having been apprenticed in 1826 to my father John Bartlett, hairdresser and brush-maker of 83 Drury Lane, a business I most heartily detested, although I used to amuse myself by preserving birds, etc., in my own private room in the house. Somewhere about 1833 or 1834 I determined again to seek the society of wild animals; but as I could not offer myself as a keeper, and as I had no means of becoming a proprietor, what was I to do? It then occurred to me that I could become a taxidermist …

'In the Exhibition of 1851 I was fortunate enough to be awarded the first prize for my specimens of taxidermy which I exhibited, viz.: eagle under glass shade, diver under glass shade (the property of

Her Majesty the Queen), snowy owl, Mandarin duck, Japanese teal, pair of Impeyan pheasants, sleeping orang-utan, sun bittern, musk deer, cockatoo, foxes; carved giraffe; two bronze medals from the Zoological Society; model of dodo; dog and deer; crowned pigeons; leopard and wolf.'

*Life among Wild Beasts in the 'Zoo', by A.D.Bartlett, 1900*

To the outside world in the latter half of the nineteenth century, A.D.Bartlett personified the Zoo. The scientific establishment of the Society was still in Hanover Square, having long since moved from Bruton Street, but Bartlett was the man in charge at Regent's Park, and many instances of his resourcefulness have been recorded:

'ICE ACCIDENT TO THE RHINOCEROS. During the hard frost of December, 1870, the Zoological Society nearly lost their rhinoceros by drowning. The animal had been turned out in the morning as usual into the paddock behind the elephant house, while the dens were being cleaned. The snow had fallen thickly during the night, so that the pond was not to be distinguished from the ground. The rhinoceros not seeing the pond put her forefeet on the ice, which immediately gave way, and in she went, head over heels with a crash. The keepers ran for Mr Bartlett; when he came, in a few minutes, he found the poor rhinoceros in great danger of drowning ... Here then was a most awkward accident, under unexpected and novel circumstances, putting Mr Bartlett's readiness of action to the test. My friend, however, with his usual courage and quickness of resource, was quite equal to the occasion. He immediately let the water off the pond by knocking away a large plug which, when the pond was originally constructed, he had thoughtfully fixed instead of a tap, a contrivance liable to get out of order ... While the water was running off, Mr Bartlett, losing no time, sent for all the available keepers and a long and strong rope; barrow loads of gravel were at the same time strewed on the sloping sides of the pond, to give the exhausted animal a foot-hold. The rope was then tossed round the haunches of the rhinoceros, like the kicking-strap of a horse in harness, and twenty-six men, one half at one end of the rope, and the other half at the other pulled hard on the rhinoceros, so that in her struggles to get up the bank she would not only be supported but pulled forcibly forwards. After much hauling on the part of the men and much plunging on the slippery bank of the pond, the rhinoceros was at last landed

'How Jumbo had his gums lanced'; Mr Bartlett operating to
remove an abscess, with an instrument fixed to a rod. *Illustrated
London News, 25 February 1882*

on terra firma. The salvors of this valuable living property had then
to look out for themselves. Mr Bartlett had anticipated this, for he
had left the sliding gate of the enclosure open just wide enough to
let out one man at a time, but not a rhinoceros. When the rhinoceros
was landed, an absurd scene took place: everybody rushed to the
gate, but the first of the fugitives, being naturally stout, and possibly
stouter at Christmas time than usual, jammed fast in the open gate,
so that the other twenty-five men were in the paddock with the
rhinoceros. The poor frightened and half-frozen beast luckily behaved very well; she did not rush after the men, but stood still,
pricked her ears and snorted, giving the keepers time to get out as

fast as they could and how they could, through the ingenious "man-hole" or guard in the railing, made in case of emergencies. Neither the rhinoceros nor the men received the slightest injury. Shortly after the accident I saw the rhinoceros munching her breakfast as if nothing had happened. This rhinoceros was the big female, which was about ten feet six inches long and about five feet high at the shoulder, and weighed at a guess between three and four tons. The ice I found was four inches thick ...

'This rhinoceros died three years afterwards, in Dec. 1873, after having lived in the Gardens for twenty-two years.'
*Logbook of a Fisherman and Zoologist, by F. Buckland, 1875*

'THE HIPPOPOTAMUS WITH THE TOOTH-ACHE. Mr Bartlett has kindly sent me the following particulars, which I am sure will be read with great interest. The operation does Mr Bartlett great credit.— F.T.BUCKLAND.—"My Dear Mr Buckland,—I had intended to write to you before I left town, but could not find time. You will be glad to know that I have succeeded in performing perhaps the largest, if not the greatest, dental operation on record. Our male hippopotamus has been, as you know, suffering from the fractured tooth, and fearing that the consequences might be serious, I have had a strong oak fence fixed between his pond and the iron railings, and I then determined to remove the broken tooth; this I accomplished on the morning of Wednesday last, but not without a fearful struggle.

A.D. Bartlett almost always wore a top hat and frock coat—even while helping nine men to move two rhinoceroses!

I had prepared a powerful pair of forceps, more than two feet long; with these I grasped his fractured incisor, thinking, with a firm and determined twist, to gain possession of that fine piece of ivory. This, however, was not quite so easily done, for the brute, amazed at my impudence, rushed back, tearing the instrument from my hands, and, looking as wild as a hippopotamus can look, charged at me just as I had recovered my forceps. I made another attempt, and this time held on long enough to cause the loose tooth to shift its position, but was again obliged to relinquish my hold. I had, however, no occasion to say, 'Open your mouth', for this he did to the fullest extent; therefore I had no difficulty in again seizing the coveted morsel, and this time drew it from his monstrous jaws. One of the most remarkable things appeared to me to be the enormous force of the air when blown from the dilated nostrils of this great beast, while enraged. It came into my face with a force that almost startled me. A.D.Bartlett."'
*Field, 10 November 1860*

'NIGHT EXPERIENCES OF ANIMALS IN THE ZOOLOGICAL GAR-
DENS. I feel that, in many respects, I resemble the ancient relative of man, Adam, living as I do, in an extensive garden surrounded by wild beasts and birds, I may say in the midst of the largest collection of wild animals on record (except the first and renowned collection in Noah's Ark), and being exhibited at the present time, in the Gardens of the Zoological Society, Regent's Park.

'Reader, for one moment kindly imagine that you are in my place, and that you have retired for the night, exhausted and tired, the result of walking, talking, thinking, being worried by endless inquiries upon inquiries, and by other incidents which happen during eighteen hours a day, and also draw on your imagination to the extent that the time of the year is the middle of August.

'You fancy everything has settled down and is at rest, and you try to sleep. All is as still as death; presently there is a soughing of the wind, the leaves begin to rustle, and this forebodes a storm.

'As the wind begins to move in anger the low, soft howl of the wolf is heard, at first difficult to distinguish from the wind; it gradually deepens, and being joined by the more harsh and distinct whining howl of the jackal and the sharp bark of the fox, the overture begins. The wolves and other denizens of the Gardens, one by one, join in the woeful concert. The hyena now and then utters a sharp laugh, while the Tasmanian devil lends his fiendish and dismal cry to render night hideous. These disturbers of the peace arouse the lions, who, no longer able to refrain, send forth their thunder, that seems like noisy smoke rolling on in volumes, and resounding in the distance renders obscure, for the moment, all other sounds.

'As the lions' voices die away the lesser din becomes more clear, and now the Polar bear tunes up, with all his might, his hoarse and savage blare, which once heard is not easily forgotten.

'Then comes a lull, and you are in hopes that they are tired now, as this band of savage vocalists has kept you on the listen for at least two hours. No! it's not over; you ask, "What horrid noise is that so close to where I lay? Have my quiet neighbours the hippopotami fallen out?" Indeed they have, and their voices seem more frightful than all the rest, because they are so unusual.'

*Life among Wild Beasts in the 'Zoo', by A.D.Bartlett, 1900*

Frank Buckland
Frank Buckland (1826–80) lived in Albany Street, Regent's Park, and was an almost daily visitor to the Zoo, where he was on good terms with A.D.Bartlett and the keepers. He was one of the most energetic of the Victorian naturalists. Starting his career as an army surgeon, he soon gave this up and devoted the rest of his life to natural history. In addition to his numerous popular writings, he became H.M. Inspector of Fisheries, and was particularly interested in the development of salmon and trout fisheries.

'The lion has a good appetite, and his principal and best-loved food is beef. Who can say that the Englishman does not resemble him in this point?

'Let us, therefore, for once go and see the lions at dinner at the Zoological Gardens, even though they are prisoners, poor beasts.*

'But we must first go into the kitchen to see the dinner prepared for the lions. Our old and civil friend William Cocksedge—who has had over thirty years' long and faithful service with the lions, and who really loves his beasts; and, if action means anything, is beloved by his beasts in turn—shows us the good things he has provided for his pets. The daily rations of the lions are alternately beef and horse; and each beast is allowed from eight to twelve pounds of meat, weighed with the bone ... Cocksedge also, from time to time, provides condiments with the meat; for upon it he occasionally sprinkles a proper allowance of common flower of brimstone, or sulphur, as this keeps the animals in good health and condition, upon the principle of occasionally giving our own youngsters a treat of brimstone-and-treacle by way of a change.'

* 'I hear there is just a possibility of a large space being enclosed at the gardens, with strong iron palisading, so as to form one gigantic cage, in which rocks, &c., will be placed; forming, in fact, a gigantic "den" for the lions. What a treat it will be to see the noble creatures in comparative freedom, and bounding about with the graceful movements peculiar to the cat tribe.' [This is now—1976—being completed.]
*Curiosities of Natural History, by F. Buckland, 1891*

Besides his more serious pursuits, which included many public lectures, Buckland took every opportunity to taste the flesh of exotic animals. 'Two young nephews called in Albany Street while he was preparing for the Brighton lecture. The old rhinoceros at the Zoological Gardens had lately died, and Frank Buckland was busy making a huge pie of a portion of the carcase, to be distributed among his Brighton audience. The nephews came in for an anticipatory share. It was like very tough beef.'
*Life of Frank Buckland, by G. C. Bompas, 1885*

Checking on the lions in Trafalgar Square ... 'SIR EDWIN LAND-SEER'S LIONS. Everyone by this time (February 1867) has seen the four lions now placed on permanent duty at the foot of Lord Nelson's column at Charing Cross, and everyone I suppose has formed his own opinion about them ... To those who think it is an easy matter to represent a lion, I would simply say, "Just try to do it. You will soon find out your mistake." It is on this account, according to my idea, that many of our friends should be very careful in giving any opinion at all as to whether Sir Edwin's lions are good or not. I candidly confess that I did not trust myself to criticize without care and painstaking; but nevertheless having in "Land and Water" promised so to do I made the attempt. In company with Mr Bartlett, the Resident Superintendent of the Zoological Gardens, who I suppose has bought and handled more lions, alive and dead, and knows more about them than any man in London, I carefully examined the details of every one of Sir Edwin's lions. We separately took

[73]

notes and mental photographs of them, and, this done, we took a Hansom's cab, and went as fast as we could straight to the Zoological Gardens, and carrying the details of the bronze lions in our mind compared them immediately with the live lions. The result is—and we trust Sir Edwin Landseer will not be offended at the course we have pursued—that we can find no fault whatever with the details, anatomical and otherwise, of his four wonderful statues. The contour and set of the ear is perfectly right. The complicated flexures of the opening nostril are true to the eighth of an inch. The twist of the lower lip, which somewhat resembles a double "S" is perfectly modelled to nature, and the tongue and teeth are quite correct. The position of the canine teeth in the heads of model lions is one of the best tests I know of painstaking observation on the part of the artist.'
*Curiosities of Natural History, by F. Buckland, 1891*

Chalmers Mitchell

Peter Chalmers Mitchell (1864–1945) was trained as a zoologist at the universities of Aberdeen and Oxford. After various teaching appointments he became Secretary of the Zoological Society in 1903, and held this, the chief executive position, until his retirement in 1935. His election as Secretary had been contested, a fairly rare occurrence in the life of a scientific society. 'A NEW SECRETARY FOR THE ZOO. Election of Dr Chalmers Mitchell. The annual general meeting of the Zoological Society was held yesterday afternoon at the Portman Rooms in Baker Street for the election of a new Secretary. The competitors were Dr P. Chalmers Mitchell and Mr W. L. Sclater, son of Dr Sclater, who held the post from 1859 until recently. We gave yesterday an account of the qualifications of both of these gentlemen.

'As anticipated, the meeting was very largely attended, among those present being the Duke of Bedford, Earl Roberts, the Marquess of Granby, Lord Avebury, Sir Harry Johnston, Dr Ray Lankester, Lord Wemyss and many other distinguished members of the Society. The Fellows of the Society voted in person, according to rule, and there was no discussion of the claims or merits of the candidates, as the letters of application and the testimonials of the candidates were circulated among the Fellows as the result of a vote passed at the monthly meeting in February last, and the discussion on the subject took place at the meeting held in March, when the candidature of Dr Chalmers Mitchell was very strongly supported by a majority of the Fellows. The Council favoured Mr Sclater, and adopted him as

'The Fellows of the Society voted in person, according to rule
... Dr Chalmers Mitchell was very strongly supported by a
majority of the Fellows.' *Daily Graphic, 30 April 1903*

their official candidate. The poll was declared at six o'clock as
follows: Dr Chalmers Mitchell, 530, Mr W.L.Sclater, 336.
   'The Duke of Bedford was re-elected President of the Society.'
*Daily Graphic, 30 April 1903*

During Mitchell's term as Secretary the number of Fellows of the
Society doubled, and the annual total of visitors to the Zoo increased
from under 700,000 to approximately two million. Many of the
animal houses were built but his greatest achievement was the
establishment of Whipsnade Park, opened in 1931.

[75]

Mitchell's retirement

'Thirty-two Years at the Zoo. Today Sir Peter Chalmers Mitchell retires from his post as Secretary of the Zoological Society of London, and that society loses the ablest and most accomplished of all those who have been the chief architects of its destiny. In his thirty-two years of service at the Zoo he introduced an order of excellence and efficiency to be found nowhere else in this or any other country. He transformed what had become little more than an "old menagerie" —and not a very prosperous one—into a place of really enthralling experience. He made himself, if anonymously, the friend of every child, and at the Zoo youth and age could meet and, hand in hand, enjoy themselves. Almost single-handed he fought the battle for light and air and freedom for the animals entrusted to his care. The Mappin Terraces, Monkey Hill, the Reptile House, the Aquarium, and Whipsnade are the spoils of his victory. Behind them all is the impulse of a mind schooled in exact knowledge, of an imagination capable of applying knowledge, and of the courage which alone can achieve when prejudice and inertia oppose. He brought science to the Zoo. But he did a greater thing than that. He brought the Zoo to science ...

'By means of the finest and most humane of all animal experiments Sir Peter Chalmers Mitchell showed that health and vigour could be increased if science's new gifts—"artificial sunlight", the oxidation of water, the control of ventilation, and conditioned air—were made available. Thus he helped forward, immeasurably, not only the cause of the well-being of animals but also that of human well-being. He recognized, too, how important so great a collection of living creatures could become as a means of studying comparative pathology. His resources were placed at the disposal of workers in this field, and indeed in all other allied fields of research, so that he gathered around him a company of workers which included the most eminent among biologists, bio-chemists, dieticians, and students of physiotherapy and tropical medicine. The studies at the Zoo have helped to save great numbers of lives—the lives of men and the lives of animals— in every part of the world. To have put happiness in the hearts of children and wisdom in the minds of men is indeed to have achieved grandly.'

*The Times, 24 April 1935*

# [3]

# Animals and Zoo

'There are badgers and bidgers and bodgers, and a
  Super-in-tendent's House,
There are masses of goats, and a Polar, and different
  kinds of mouse,
And I think there's a sort of a something which is
  called a wallaboo—
But *I* gave buns to the elephant when I went down to
  the Zoo!'
*When we were very young, by A. A. Milne, 1924*

> Homo sapiens
> MAN

'This specimen, born in Scotland, was presented to the
Society by John Cromartie, Esq. Visitors are requested
not to irritate the Man by personal remarks.'
*A Man in the Zoo, by David Garnett, 1924*

Jane, the first orang-utan. A lithograph of 1837 by George Scharf

# [3]
# Animals and Zoo

### Animals famous and otherwise

Over the last 150 years many thousands of animals from elephants, mice, birds and snakes, to lobsters, octopus and locusts have been exhibited in the Society's collections. The majority of these have provided the background to the Society's activities, whether as exhibits or as objects of scientific study. Some individual animals, however, have become public characters and their names have become household words. Such are Jumbo the African elephant, Jubilee the first chimpanzee born in London and Chi-Chi the giant panda of our own times.

### An early escape

'MENAGERIE: All animals well. Received an Angola Cat from Bruton Street. Emu laid her eighth egg ... SERVANTS: Assistant keeper gone to St Albans for Badgers etc. ...'
*Occurrences, 17 March 1828*

'MENAGERIE: All animals well ... The Angola Cat stray'd away and has not yet been found ... MISCELLANEOUS REPORT: Found the body of a leveret which it is supposed was killed by a cat, probably the Angola Cat.'
*Occurrences, 21 March 1828*

### Jane, the first orang-utan, 1837

'This interesting specimen of the Asiatic orang-utan, (a female rejoicing in the pretty cognomen of "Jane") was purchased of her importer by the Zoological Society, and added to their menagerie about a month since. A keeper has been appointed by the Council to attend exclusively to her accommodation: so that, were she an Asiatic princess, her comfort could not be more specially studied. She is supposed to be about four years old; her height, when erect, is somewhat over two feet; her ears are much admired for their smallness and neatness. She is very docile and quiet, and thus distinguished from the mischievous monkey tribe.

'From the *Magazine of Natural History* for the present month, we

[79]

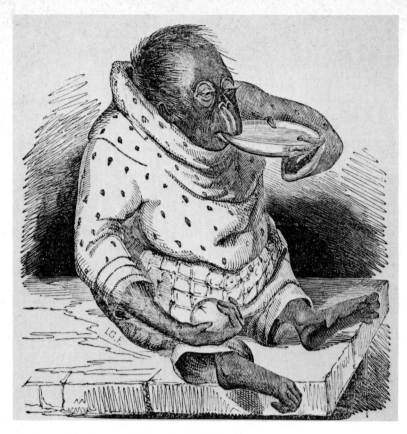

Jane 'is very docile and quiet'. *The Mirror, 13 January 1838*

learn that the orang has become excessively attached to her keeper, and is daily improving in strength and spirits, and promises to be, for a long time, one of the most attractive objects at the Gardens. At the evening meeting of the Zoological Society, 12 Dec., Mr Owen made some remarks upon one or two particulars, in which this animal differs very materially from the chimpanzee, whose death was so much regretted about two years since. He observed, that one very marked difference consisted in the inferiority of the orang, as regards the functions of the organs of voice; for, while the chimpanzee expressed its anger by loud cries, or a succession of short, quick sounds, resembling a bark, the orang, when vexed or thwarted of its favourite object, displayed its wrath by uttering a feeble and almost inaudible continuous whine. The orang is far less active in its habits, rarely moving, unless to follow its keeper, or when strongly tempted,

and then its motion is slower, and more awkward than in the chimpanzee; the awkwardness arising from the extreme disparity in the length of the anterior and posterior extremities. The hair on the head is all directed forwards; in the chimpanzee it radiated from a centre. Mr Owen also remarked that the thumbs of the lower extremities were devoid of nails, and that the animal had the deciduous series of teeth in use; viz. two canines and four grinders in each jaw.'
*The Mirror, 13 January 1838*

Jenny, the second orang-utan
Jenny was much admired by the great anatomist, Richard Owen, in 1842. 'During the fine weather Owen and his wife were both constant visitors at the Zoological Gardens. Of their special favourite, Jenny the orang-utan, Mrs Owen wrote: "We saw Jenny have her cup of tea again. It was spooned and sipped in the most ladylike way, and Hunt, the keeper, put a very smart cap on her head, which made it all the more laughable. Hunt told me that, a few days ago, the Queen and Prince Albert were highly amused with Jenny's tricks, but that he did not like to put the cap on Jenny, as he was afraid it might be thought vulgar!"'
*The Life of Richard Owen, by Richard Owen, 1894*

Obaysch, the first hippopotamus, 1850
'The hippopotamus. (*Hippopotamus amphibius.*) The fact of hippopotami having been on many occasions exhibited by the emperor of Rome in the great displays of wild beasts which were presented to the people in the circus, was a sufficient proof that the animal could be transported from its haunts in the Nile with success. And, therefore, although 1,500 years had elapsed since the last recorded instance of this kind, the Council of the Zoological Society, in the year 1849, undertook, with considerable confidence, the operation of obtaining one from Upper Egypt, all attempts to obtain it on the west coast having proved futile.

'By the influence of the Hon. C. A. Murray, then H.M. Agent and Consul-General at Cairo, His Highness the Viceroy, Abbas Pasha, was induced to give orders that this object should be effected; and in the month of July in that year [1849] a party of hunters, specially organized for the purpose, succeeded in capturing a calf of some three days' old on the island of Obaysch, in the White Nile.'
*Guide to the Gardens, 1882*

'Read letters addressed to the Secretary by the Hon. C. A. Murray, dated Cairo 16 Dec. 1849, in which he announces that H.H. Abbas Pasha had presented to him for the Society a young living hippopotamus, a lioness and a cheetah. This important letter ... suggested that a present of greyhounds should be transmitted to the Viceroy of Egypt with the least possible delay, as a proof of the Society's appreciation of His Highness' great liberality, which was not confined to the gifts above mentioned as actually in the possession of Mr Murray, but extended to the promise of a female hippopotamus also, in quest of which a party of troops were still out by His Highness' orders on the White Nile.'
*Minutes, 19 December 1849*

'The Secretary was authorized to make the necessary arrangements with the Peninsular and Oriental Steam Navigation Company for the accommodation of the hippopotamus on board the steamer, *Ripon*, and to order a tank and other fittings to be executed by the Company's workmen at Southampton.'
*Minutes, 3 April 1850*

Professor Owen publishes a note on Obaysch
'The young hippopotamus was safely housed in the comfortable quarters prepared for it at the Zoological Gardens about 10 o'clock on Saturday night (25 May), having arrived by special train from Southampton, where it was landed from the *Ripon* steamer which reached that port early in the morning. The strong attachment of the animal to its keeper removed every difficulty in its various transfers from ship to train, and from wagon to its actual abode. On arriving at the Gardens, the Arab who has had the charge of it walked first out of the transport van, with a bag of dates over his shoulder, and the beast trotted after him, now and then lifting up its huge grotesque muzzle and sniffing at its favourite dainties, with which it was duly rewarded on entering its apartment. When I saw the hippopotamus the next morning, it was lying on its side in the straw with its head resting against the chair on which its swarthy attendant sat; it now and then uttered a soft complacent grunt, and, lazily opening its thick smooth eyelids, leered at its keeper with a singular protruding movement of the eyeball from the prominent socket, showing an unusual proportion of the white, over which large conjunctival vessels converged to the margin of the cornea. The retraction of the eyeball is

Obaysch arrived by steamer with his Arab keeper from the
White Nile in 1850. *Illustrated London News, 1 June 1850*

accompanied by a protrusion of a large and thick "palpebra nictitans",
and by a simultaneous rolling of the ball obliquely downwards and
inwards or forwards.'
*Annals of Natural History, 1850*

Obaysch escapes
'Many were Frank Buckland's stories of the Zoological Gardens.
One was how Obaysch, the first hippopotamus, once got loose. It
was early in the morning, before the Gardens were opened, when a
keeper rushed into Mr Bartlett's house, exclaiming "Obaysch is
out!" and, sure enough, there came Obaysch down the long walk,
his huge mouth curled into a ghastly smile, as if he meant mischief.
The cunning brute had contrived to push back the door of his den,
while his keeper had gone for the carpenter to mend some defect
in it. Having warned everyone to keep out of the way, Mr Bartlett
called his keeper, who tried to coax the hippopotamus back with
sweet hay. The brute munched the hay, but showed no sign of going
back. What was to be done? Mr Bartlett is a man of unfailing resource.

[83]

There was one keeper Obaysch hated, and ran at him whenever he came in sight. "Scott," said Mr Bartlett, putting a bank note in his hand, "throw open the paddock gate, and then show yourself to Obaysch at the end of the path, and run for it." The man looked at the note, and then through the trees at the beast, and, going into the middle of the path, shouted defiantly "Obaysch." Ugh! roared the beast, viciously, and wheeling his huge carcase suddenly round, rushed with surprising swiftness after the keeper. Scott ran for his life; with the hippopotamus roaring at his heels, into the paddock and over the palings, Obaysch close to his coat-tails; bang slammed the gate, and the monster was caged again. Just then, up drove a cab with a newspaper reporter. "I hear," he said, "the hippopotamus is loose!" "Oh dear no," innocently replied Mr Bartlett, "he is safe in his den; come and see."'
*Life of Frank Buckland*, by G.C. Bompas, *1885*

Obaysch's obituary
'THE ZOOLOGICAL GARDENS. The Fellows and friends of the Zoological Society of London will hear with regret of the death of the old hippopotamus, which occurred on Monday afternoon, rather suddenly, but not unexpectedly, as he had been showing manifest signs of old age for some time. "Obaysch" was born in the White Nile, somewhere near the island whence he obtained his name, in the spring of 1849, and was captured when about three days old by a party of hunters sent out by Abbas Pasha, then Viceroy of Egypt, for the purpose. From the White Nile he was conveyed down to Cairo, and passed the winter in a tank specially built for him within the British Agency, under the care of the Hon. Sir C. Murray, then Her Majesty's Consul-General for Egypt. On 25 May, 1850, he made his triumphal entry into London by special train of the South-Western Railway, and has since remained an inmate of the house prepared for his reception in the Zoological Society's Gardens. In 1853 his mate Adhela was acquired from the same country, but though several infant hippos were the result of this union, only one of them lived to attain maturity—a female born on Guy Fawkes day, 1872, and now living in the gardens. Last year the Council, seeing that "Obaysch" was well stricken in years, thought it advisable to secure a mate for the youthful Guy Fawkes, and with that object purchased of the Zoological Society of Amsterdam a young male hippopotamus, born in their gardens on 30 June last. There is, therefore, every prospect

of the race of British hippopotami being continued in future years. The post-mortem examination of the old hippopotamus was commenced yesterday by Professor Garrod, F.R.S., the prosector of the Society, with several volunteer assistants to aid him in his formidable task. Professor Garrod will communicate the results to the Society at one of their next scientific meetings.'
*The Times, 13 March 1878*

Help from the Empire
'To offer the best thanks of the Society to Major John Pearse, Madras Staff Corps, for his acceptable present of a Black Leopard.'
*Minutes, 18 September 1867*

Dear pheasants
'To purchase two male Amherst Pheasants, now deposited in the Gardens, for the sum of £120.' [These birds would now be valued at only £5–£6 a pair.]
*Minutes, 15 March 1871*

Early attempts to procure an African elephant
'That the Secretary be directed to write to Dr Livingstone and authorize him to offer £150 on the part of the Society for the first elephant, and £150 for the first rhinoceros, brought down fit for shipment at Quillimane, and £100 for the second animal of each species, provided it be of the opposite sex.'
*Minutes, 3 February 1858*

The arrival of Jumbo, 1865
'The first elephant that ever came immediately under my charge was the celebrated "Jumbo".

   'The African elephant "Jumbo" was received in exchange for other animals on 26 June 1865.

   'At that date he was about four feet high and he was in a filthy and miserable condition. I handed him over to Matthew Scott, who I thought was the most likely man to attend to my instructions because he had no previous experience in the treatment and management of elephants. The first thing was to endeavour to remove the accumulated filth and dirt from his skin. This was a task requiring a considerable amount of labour and patience, and was not to be done in the space of a moment … We coaxed him and fed him with a few tempting

The African elephant, Jumbo. *Illustrated London News, 15 July, 1865*

morsels, and after this time he appeared to recognize that we were
his best friends, and he continued on the best of terms with both of
us until about the year before he was sold. He was at that time about
twenty-one years old and had attained the enormous size of nearly
eleven feet in height. As I have before mentioned, all male elephants
at this age and in this condition become troublesome and dangerous.
"Jumbo" was no exception to this rule. He commenced to destroy
the doors and other parts of his house, driving his tusks through the
iron plates, splintering the timber in all directions, rendering it
necessary to have the house propped up, as it still remains, with
massive timber beams ... "Jumbo" had been for nearly sixteen
years quiet, gentle, and tractable, and had been daily in the habit of
carrying hundreds of visitors about the gardens. Finding that he, at
. the end of this period, was likely to do some fatal mischief I made an
application to the Council to be supplied with a sufficiently powerful

rifle in the event of finding it necessary to kill him. Strange to say also about this time I received a letter from the late Mr Barnum, asking if the Society would sell the big African elephant, and, if so, at what price. I submitted Mr Barnum's letter to the Council, and was instructed to dispose of the animal for £2,000. I wrote immediately to Mr Barnum telling him that he could have "Jumbo" for £2,000 "as he stands", my object being to save the Society the expense of packing and forwarding this huge animal to America. Mr Barnum replied by telegram—"I accept your offer; my agents will be with you in a few days."'

*Wild Animals in Captivity*, by A.D.Bartlett, *1898*

The public becomes alarmed

'Can nothing be done to rescue Jumbo, "the great and docile elephant", as a correspondent in *The Times* describes him, "who has for so many years been one of the chief attractions of the Zoological Gardens, but who, for reasons difficult to understand, has lately been sold to an American showman"? What Jumbo himself thinks of his change of prospects is only too pathetically certain. He won't go. To every attempt to inveigle or force him he opposes an intelligent, patient, resolute resistance, and, as he happens to weigh six tons, the element of *vis inertia* in his case is plainly considerable. Jumbo is evidently as unwilling to part with his London friends as they, if they have any

THE ROUTE TO MILLWALL.

Now through streets I slowly go, while my poor heart is full of woe.
And to each child I see in grief I fondly wave my handkerchief.
And weep that I shall see no more their rosy cheeks on Albion's shore

sense or feeling, will be desolate at the thought of losing him. Is this the way we recompense our oldest friends, those best benefactors who have given us the one boon which is without alloy—hearty and innocent enjoyment? After all the children he has so patiently carried, all the buns he has so quietly and graciously received, is he to be turned out at last to tramp the world homeless and unbefriended, the mere chattel of a wandering showman? What a reward for old and tried service! What a commentary on our pennyworths of insincere affection! It is surely not too much to hope that the doom of Jumbo will yet be reversed, and that the only effect of the whole proceeding will be to have spread far and wide the name and fame of his present owner, Mr Barnum. We do not grudge that gentleman his notoriety; but he ought to be satisfied with it and to consent to surrender the animal, the temporary ownership of which has probably made his fortune.'
*Pall Mall Gazette, 21 February 1882*

Why part with Jumbo?
'The Secretary laid before the Council a memorial from W.E. Milliken, Esq. and a large number of signers petitioning against the removal of the male African elephant. It was agreed that the memorial should be returned to Mr Milliken, and that he should be informed that it had been laid before the Council.'
*Minutes, 5 April 1882*

The Society explains …
'ZOOLOGICAL SOCIETY OF LONDON. It is not surprising to the Council of this Society that so general a regret should have been expressed by visitors to our gardens at the prospect of losing the great African elephant. It is quite certain that the members of the Council of the Society share in this regret as much as any of the Fellows, and that they would not have consented to part with the animal unless satisfactory reasons for so doing had been placed before them by the responsible executive of the gardens. It was, however, hoped that the Fellows of the Society and others would have been satisfied that the Council were acting for the best, and would not have required any detailed statement of the motives by which the Council were guided in this transaction. Quiet and tractable as this fine animal generally seems to be, he has for some time been a source of anxiety to those in charge of him. It is well known to all who have had much experience with such animals in confinement

IN AMERICAN COSTUME.

And when the Yankees saw my size, they opened their astonished eyes.
The gents with pride puffed at their pipes and dressed me up with stars and stripes
While joy-bells rang and ladies smiled and every child with joy was wild

that male elephants, when they arrive at the adult stage, are periodically liable to fits of uncertain temper. Under these circumstances the risk of an outbreak on the part of so huge and powerful an animal in the much-frequented gardens of the Society is not one which should be lightly run. The possibility of having to destroy the animal would be repugnant to the feelings of all who know and admire him, especially as there seems to be no reason whatever to suppose that when once the removal is over he may not be well cared for and live comfortably. Messrs Barnum, Bailey, and Hutchinson are understood to have upwards of twenty elephants in their possession. That the circumstances under which these animals are kept are very favourable is proved by the fact that already two young ones have been born among them, an occurrence hitherto unprecedented in captivity. In so large an establishment any animal under temporary excitement can be withdrawn from exhibition and placed in seclusion, which there are no adequate means of doing in the gardens in the Regent's Park.

'After this explanation it is hoped that the Fellows of this Society and visitors to the Gardens will feel that the Council have not been unmindful of their interests, or even of those of Jumbo himself, when they, though very reluctantly, consented to part with him. P.L. Sclater, Secretary. 11 Hanover Square, London, W. 21 February, 1882.'

First attempts to crate Jumbo
'Today commences the formidable task of getting the elephant Jumbo into the huge box which has been constructed for the purpose of carrying him across the Atlantic. Should he raise any objection, as is not unlikely, the first stage in his removal will be one of the most interesting scenes that has been witnessed at the Zoological Gardens for some years.

'The box arrived at Regent's Park yesterday. It is constructed of strong planking, soundly bolted together, and clamped with iron. Its weight is about eight tons. The lower part of each end is simply barred across, so that Jumbo will have considerable liberty for his trunk; but otherwise he will be closely and strongly confined. The box is placed on a very heavy trolley, one end of which has been lowered into the ground so that the ascent may be more easy.'
*Echo, 18 February 1882*

'The following instructions to be given by the Secretary to the Superintendent relative to the removal of the male African elephant were approved of:
'"You will give Mr Barnum's agents every reasonable assistance in packing and moving out of the Gardens the male African elephant. But this must be done in the presence of the agents of the Society for the Prevention of Cruelty to Animals, and in case of their inter-ference you are to withdraw all assistance immediately. Mr Davis on the part of Mr Barnum assents to this arrangement." '
*Minutes, 15 March 1882*

Postscript on Jumbo
'THE ORIGIN OF THE NAME "JUMBO". The word "Jumbo" has so completely entered into our language that it is included in the dic-tionaries, but even the Oxford Dictionary does not make any suggestion about its origin. I submit, therefore, the following, which seems to me very probable. In several Bantu languages the word for elephant is *Njamba*, or something very close to it. That is the case in Chokwe or Chibokwe, and readers of Livingstone may remember that he had

trouble with a chief of that name. I had a gun boy in Angola, of the same tribe, also of that name, and I believe the word is the same in the Umbundu group of languages. As Jumbo was an African elephant, this seems to me to be a very probable origin of the name. Malcolm Burr.'
*Zoo Life, Winter 1948*

Russel Wallace sends Birds of Paradise
Alfred Russel Wallace (1823–1913), a distinguished naturalist who collected zoological material in the Amazon region and the Malay Archipelago, was in 1858 the joint author with Charles Darwin of a paper putting forward the principle of natural selection as a factor in evolution.

'The following resolutions were also agreed to, viz.: That Mr Wallace's terms for supplying Birds of Paradise to be delivered living in London at the following rates, should be accepted, viz., £100 for the first Bird, £50 for the second, £25 each for the third and others up to ten.'
*Minutes, 17 August 1859*

'It was proposed by J.H. Gurney, Esq. M.P., and unanimously agreed to: That the sum of £307.9.0 (being £150 for the Birds, £137.3.0 for his passage from Singapore to London, and £20.6.0 for Sundry Expenses) should be paid to Mr Wallace for the two Paradise Birds.'
*Minutes, 16 April 1862*

The first live gorilla
'For the first time since the establishment of the Gardens of the Zoological Society a living gorilla has been added to the collection. It is a young animal, but as little is known of the life-history of these creatures, so rarely seen in captivity, and as it brought no certificate of birth with it from its native land, it is impossible to give more than a guess at its exact age. Although it has been scarcely a month in the gardens it is rapidly recovering from the shyness before strangers which it exhibited at first, and it feeds freely on almost every kind of fruit offered to it, showing a marked preference, however, for pomegranates ...'
*Illustrated London News, 10 November 1887*

The first gorilla. *Illustrated London News, 12 November 1887*

The chimpanzee Sally dies, 1891
'The Zoological Gardens have sustained a serious bereavement in
the death of Sally, the black-faced chimpanzee from the west coast
of the Gaboon, who for eight years has entertained many thousands
of folk of all ages and of both sexes at the popular Gardens in Regent's
Park. The intelligence of Sally has been the subject of comment amongst
men of science, of sages and philosophers, and possibly theologians.
Perhaps the most remarkable of her feats was that of counting. Sally,
in the presence of a crowded room, when called upon, say for bits of
the straw in her cage, would give you the exact number you named,
up to ten, and the keeper has found her when alone count in this way
up to twenty. If one of the public asked for five, six, or nine straws,
or whatever quantity up to ten, she would pick each deliberately up,

without any mistake, put one by one in her mouth until all were got together, and then give them into your hand. If asked for a "button-hole", she would take a straw, break off part of the stalk, and put the ear into the button-hole of the keeper's coat. She knew right from left; would use a spoon, and sip with it until the cup was empty. She was four years old when first brought to this country, and was therefore twelve years of age. Though seeming to understand almost all that was going on round her, she could never frame any articulate speech. Her memoir deserves to be written by someone who is qualified by intimate acquaintance. Unlike most other biographers, he will have nothing to conceal. Poor Sally's death has been previously reported, but it actually took place on Friday last.'

*Daily News, 31 August 1891*

Sally, the chimpanzee from the west coast of the Gaboon.
*Daily News, 31 August 1891*

The first birth of a chimpanzee at Regent's Park
'SPECIALIST VISITS BOO-BOO ... (By our Zoo Correspondent.)
An obstetric surgeon, probably for the first time in history, is in
attendance on a chimpanzee.

'The specialist is Mr James Wyatt, obstetric surgeon to St Thomas's
Hospital, London, and he paid two visits to the Zoo yesterday to
observe the progress of Boo-Boo, at the birth of whose baby, Jubilee,
he was present on Friday.

'"As the birth of a chimpanzee is the nearest approach among
animals to the birth of a human being, I was very interested from a
professional standpoint," said Mr Wyatt, who is a close friend of
Dr Vevers, the Zoo Superintendent.

'"The event was so noteworthy that Dr Vevers and I are to col-
laborate in a paper which we shall read to a special meeting of the
Zoological Society."'
*Daily Mail, 17 February 1935*

Kruger's lion
'That the special thanks of the Society be offered to the Rt. Hon
Cecil J. Rhodes, P.C., D.C.L., F.Z.S., for his acceptable present of a
lioness.'
*Minutes, 15 August 1900*

'It will be remembered that just before the outbreak of the war
Mr Rhodes presented the Pretoria Zoological Gardens with a young
lion, and that Mr Kruger, in high dudgeon, ordered the immediate
return of the gift.

'Mr Rhodes subsequently sent the animal to London, where it
found a home in Regent's Park.

'With the changed conditions of things in the Transvaal, however,
Pretoria is anxious to have the lion back again, and it is said that
Mr Rhodes will be approached with that object. The Zoo is willing.'
*Daily Mail, 10 January 1902*

'That the request of the executors of the late Mr Rhodes, F.Z.S.,
asking the Society to return to the Zoological Gardens at Pretoria the
lioness called "Kruger's Lion", presented to the Society by Mr Rhodes,
be granted.'
*Minutes, 7 May 1902*

Mr Thomson brought back Colonel Mahon's giraffes from
Cairo: one of them went to Dublin, and two to Regent's Park.
*The Sphere, 6 September 1902*

Zebras and giraffes

'The Secretary reported that, at the request of Lord Lansdowne, he
had sent keeper George Blore to Aden by the S.S. *Goorkha*, which
had left London on 16 May, to fetch home some zebras presented by
the Emperor Menelik to the King. It was hoped that Blore would be
able to return by the British India Steamship leaving Aden on 21 June
which would reach London on 12 July.

'The Secretary had interviewed Col. Mahon, and had arranged to
send Mr Arthur Thomson, the Assistant Superintendent to Cairo
by the B.I.S.S. *Golconda*, leaving on the 30th inst, and arriving at

[95]

Port Said on 13 June to fetch the pair of giraffes presented by that gentleman. It was hoped that Mr Thomson would be able to catch at Port Said (on 27 June) the same steamer as Blore would take with the zebras, and arrive home on 12 July.'
*Minutes, 21 May 1902*

The gorilla, John Daniel
'A letter having been read from Miss Alyse Cunningham, it was agreed to accept her offer to exhibit her gorilla daily at the Gardens during the Season, Miss Cunningham to provide food and an attendant, and to bring and take back the ape every day. The Secretary was empowered to treat with her on these lines up to a sum of £30 a week.'
*Minutes, 6 May 1925*

'Arising from the Minutes the Secretary reported that he had arranged with Miss Cunningham for showing the gorilla at a rate of £23 per week.'
*Minutes, 20 May 1925*

Miss Cunningham's gorilla, John Daniel, in August 1919

And on 5 November 1947 the Zoo received a male gorilla, about one and a half years old, and weighing only 10.635 kg. This animal, named Guy after the date of his arrival, now weighs about 200 kg, and is one of the best-known Zoo characters.

'The zoo favours a scientific approach and frowns on sentimentality. But Mr Callard softens when you mention Guy the gorilla, who arrived in a little wooden box on 5 November, 1947, clutching a tin hot-water bottle.

'"We used to wrestle with him until he started wanting the games to go on and we had to rescue the Head Keeper." ...

'"He's great, is Guy. He scorns most people. He is a very superior person.

' "Yet if a sparrow flew into his old cage he would scoop it up into his great hands and squat there peering at it through his fingers, then let it go. He never kills them.

'"The other apes catch sparrows and eat them, but I think he knows how little and weak they are compared with him."'
*Daily Mail, 7 October 1974*

Early TV stars
'It was also agreed after discussion to lend to the British Broadcasting Corporation for two hours on an evening in July the following for an experiment in combined broadcasting and television, the Garden Committee having reported that there seemed no danger to the animals for which permission was given. The animals were to be accompanied to Broadcasting House by their keepers: Mynah, White cockatoo—Cocky, Black-crested parrot, Black macaw—Nigger, Blue macaw, with black-and-white face—Markus, Small Senegal parrot, Hornbill, Toucan, West African python, Boa constrictor, Monkey—Charlie, Small alligator.'
*Minutes, 21 June 1933*

The escape of Cholmondeley the chimp
'Cholmondeley was brought to the Zoo in 1948, when he was eight years old. It was on 9 January 1951, that Cholmondeley ran away, boarded a 53 bus in Albany Street, and hugged Mrs Felicity Chilcott, of Cumberland-terrace Mews, N.W.—and then bit her.'
*Daily Express, 27 December 1951*

The escape of Goldie in 1965

'In the early part of 1965 there happened in Britain a small, and apparently insignificant event. As a result of it the nation demonstrated to the world that it was even more queer in the head than had been generally suspected.

'For almost a whole fortnight the people of Britain appeared to become obsessed by one single solitary bird. This bird was an eagle that had escaped from the London Zoo and during the time that it was free, between the dates of February 27 and March 11, some very odd things happened in Britain with regard to it.

'The eagle was seen on the television screens of the British people more than a hundred times. News of it was given out by the British Broadcasting Corporation in sixty-five bulletins on the Home, Light and Third networks. Only a few days after its escape it had become front-page headlines in all the daily papers. The Zoo was receiving non-stop deliveries of letters—over a thousand of them—telephone calls, telegrams and parcels of meat and other oddments, besides a constant stream of visitors who called with the express purpose of giving their views on, or offering to help with the capture, of the eagle. When reference was made to it in the House of Commons, the bird was cheered wildly by Members of Parliament. On one single day alone traffic jams were caused in and about Regent's Park when *five thousand* people came to look at the eagle and pursue it as it flew from tree to tree.

'The eagle came to be called "Goldie". This name had to be hastily thought up for the inquiring press by one of the Zoo's officials, as the bird population at the Zoo is too numerous for them all to have individual pet names. But it was a good name, and in spite of—or because of—its banality, the British took it to their hearts at once. They loved and cherished it, with humour and great affection, just as they had done, for almost twenty years, the names of Mrs Dale and Dan and Doris Archer, the leading figures in their two long-running radio soap-operas.

'Goldie's adventures became, in themselves, a soap-opera, and were followed avidly by the public from day to day. As a result of all this strange behaviour on the part of the sober-minded English, he became internationally famous.

'He was described, rather grandly, by the *Daily Mail* as—"the most celebrated eagle of our day".'

*Eaglemania, by Jonquil Antony, 1965*

'Cet aigle se moque de 8 millions d'Anglais: tous les Londoniens. Evadé du Zoo depuis lundi dernier, il se promène insolemment à travers la Cité, avec une préférence marquée pour les beaux quartiers. "Bobies" et pompiers sont mobilisés nuit et jour pour le capturer. Mais "Goldie", 1,80 mètre d'envergure, a déjoué toutes les ruses. Du haut de son arbre, il nargue l'orgueilleuse Albion.'
*Paris Match, 13 March 1965*

Giant Pandas
Giant Pandas started arriving in zoos in the 1930s and have always been popular with the public. In recent years the most famous one at London was Chi-Chi who arrived in 1958.

The death of Chi-Chi
'On 22 July, there was a less happy but nevertheless momentous day when the Giant Panda "Chi-Chi" died after nearly fourteen years in the Zoo. She had, so far as is known, lived longer than any other Giant Panda in captivity, and during this time some 25,000,000 people would have seen her. She takes her place with other London Zoo historical animals such as Jumbo, the famous elephant of Victorian

days, and Jubilee, the chimpanzee which was born in 1935.'
*Annual Report, 1972*

Ching-Ching and Chia-Chia
And then in 1974 came Ching-Ching and Chia-Chia, a gift from the
Chinese Government ... 'On the occasion of the Rt Hon. Edward
Heath's visit to China in June 1974, the Chinese Government made
a gift of two Giant Pandas to the British people. Ching-Ching, the
female, whose name means "Crystal Bright", and Chia-Chia, "Most
Excellent and Very Best", were both born in the autumn of 1972 ...
In order that the animals would not have to travel in the heat of the
day, the flight to London was altered so that the plane flew across
India and the Persian Gulf at night. As an extra precaution, air-
conditioning units were provided at the refuelling stops at Hong
Kong, Calcutta and Dubai. The pandas ate and slept on the twenty-
hour journey, and were greeted by over forty photographers at
London Airport. They made their debut the next day, 15 September,
before an excited crowd. Once out in their new paddock, all caution
vanished and they put on a "show" of sheer panda playfulness.'
*The Society's Notes on the Giant Panda, 1975*

But when an earlier Giant Panda arrived in 1946 there was no danger
of jetlag ... 'Hullo Children. First of all I am going to tell you something about Lien-Ho, the baby Giant Panda which arrived at the
Zoo just over a week ago. Her name—Lien-Ho—is Chinese, and in
English means "Union", and she is a symbol of unity between two
great nations, the Chinese and the British. She came from the moun-
tain slopes of Szechuan, a province of South Western China, and had
been presented to the Zoo by the Government of that Province. Her
travels began when she was taken to Chengtu, the capital of Szechuan,
and put in the care of Professor Ma Teh, who looked after her on the
long, but very quick journey of over 7,000 miles from China, which
took only six days. From Chengtu the panda was flown to Chungking,
then to Calcutta, and from Calcutta to an aerodrome in Dorset. She
then went by train to London and finished her journey to the Zoo in
a British Overseas Airways van ...'
*Talk by Geoffrey Vevers, BBC Children's Hour, 20 May 1946*

## Care and health

The care of animals kept in captivity has been a constant concern of the Society throughout its history. Some of the methods used in the nineteenth century may appear rather crude to us these days, but even human medicine was fairly primitive at that time.

Today, the Society has an excellently equipped Animal Hospital, with a fully qualified veterinary and animal-nursing staff.

### The first medical attendant

'Mr Sabine reported that it having been suggested that the services of a regular medical attendant, under the direction of Mr Sewell, would be of advantage at the Gardens, he had consulted with Mr Sewell on the subject; who had recommended Mr Charles Spooner, of Cook's Row, Camden Town, as fitted for the purpose: That he had seen and conferred with Mr Spooner, who was willing to engage on the duty on trial, his payment being after the rate of £60 per annum, to attend three times in each week, and oftener when necessary, to prescribe for and examine all the animals; and to keep a record of his observations and practice, and to report the same. It was ordered that Mr Spooner be engaged on trial.'
*Minutes, 1 July 1829*

In 1833 William Youatt was appointed Medical Superintendent, a post he held until his death in 1847. 'The Medical Superintendent shall attend on a Monday and on a Thursday, when the Head Keeper if at home, will accompany him in a general inspection of the whole menagerie. In the absence of the Head Keeper the Assistant Keeper in charge will act as Head Keeper. On these visits the Medical Superintendent will give his directions as to the treatment of all ailing animals. The administering the medicines and performing operations to be done by himself, or in his presence if he thinks necessary, otherwise, or in his absence by or in the presence of, or under the orders of the Head Keeper ...

'An apartment with a supply of instruments and medicines is provided for the use of the Medical Superintendent, where he will record his observations and proceedings and keep his journals. Such alterations or improvement in this place as will make it convenient for the Medical Superintendent's purposes, will be allowed by the Council.

'The Medical Superintendent will on all occasions be required in

Shifting the lions to the new Lion House, 1876

case of the death of any animal to ascertain the cause of its death by
post-mortem examination ...'
*Minutes, 22 May 1833*

Good management
'In 1876 the Lion House was finished, and early in the year the larger
*Felidae* were removed to their new dens. The transfer of the animals
excited a good deal of interest, and Mr Bartlett, the Superintendent,
received a number of suggestions as to how this could best be accomplished. It was, however, effected in a very simple manner. The
animals, one by one, were enticed into travelling boxes by food placed
at the far end. As each entered what was practically a trap, a keeper
told off for the duty dropped the sliding door behind it. The bell was
then rung, the keepers gathered together on the Terrace, the travelling
den was wheeled to the Lion House, and its occupant safely deposited
in its new home. The operation of shifting was necessarily somewhat

slow; but it was managed without the slightest accident to man or beast. At the date of the anniversary there were in the new house six lions, seven tigers, two jaguars, two leopards, three pumas, and one Clouded tiger—twenty-one in all.'

*Record of the Progress of the Zoological Society of London during the Nineteenth Century, by P.L.Sclater, 1901*

Food for the animals in 1895

'Much interest being taken in the way in which the 2,500 animals usually living in the Menagerie are fed, the Council have had compiled the subjoined table of the provisions purchased for them in 1895:

| | | | |
|---|---|---|---|
| Clover Hay | $113\frac{1}{4}$ loads | Goats | 197 |
| Meadow Hay | 131 loads | Flounders | 2,184 lbs |
| Oats | 144 qrs | Whiting | 26,520 lbs |
| Wheat | $43\frac{1}{2}$ qrs | Shrimps | 1,252 quarts |
| Maize | 70 qrs | Fowl-heads | 7,512 |
| Bran | 350 qrs | Rough Fish | 9,667 lbs |
| Canary | 15 qrs | Greens | 37 bush. |
| Hemp | $11\frac{3}{4}$ qrs | Cabbage | 260 doz. |
| Rape | 1 qr | Onions | 3 bush. |
| Millet | $3\frac{3}{4}$ qrs | Watercress | 3,436 bunches |
| Barley | $28\frac{1}{4}$ qrs | Nuts | $33\frac{1}{2}$ pks |
| Bread | 5,515 qtns | Lettuce | 229 doz. |
| Biscuits | 302 cwt | Apples | 138 bush. |
| Rice | 78 cwt | Pears | $2\frac{1}{2}$ bush. |
| Oil-cake | 56 cwt | Grapes | 1,156 lbs |
| Mawseed | 28 cwt | Dates | 1,395 lbs |
| Buckwheat | 6 qrs | Oranges | 169 hundreds |
| Ground Nuts | 29 cwt | Carrots | 132 cwt |
| Barley Meal | 3 cwt | Potatoes | 59 cwt |
| Oatmeal | 2 cwt | Cherries | 9 boxes |
| Milk | 5,120 qts | Marrows | 35 doz. |
| Eggs | 23,954 | Bananas | 1,149 doz. |
| Horses | 200 | Melons | 50 |

*Annual Report, 1895*

Chloroforming a tiger

'ZOO'S OPERATION ON RAJAH. Rajah the Zoo's famous tiger ... was chloroformed and operated upon yesterday.

'The operation was the removal of an in-growing claw, which was piercing the flesh of his left paw and was causing him pain.

'The big chloroform box in which sick animals on occasion are anaesthetized in order to be cured of their troubles had stood in

Rajah's sleeping den for some time, so that he could get accustomed to it and overcome all his suspicions.

'Yesterday morning Hopgood, the Head Keeper—with whom Rajah is on the best of terms—persuaded Rajah to go into the chloroform chamber and lie down.

'The door was then securely clamped, the box was wheeled to the front of Rajah's cage, the chloroform was pumped in gently, and in a few moments Rajah dropped quietly into unconsciousness.

'The door was lifted an inch or two and Dr Vevers, Superintendent of the Zoo, clipped the offending claw off neatly and gently.

'A few moments later Rajah recovered consciousness, walked slowly out of the box, a little bit dazed, perhaps, and went straight into his sleeping den for a pleasant nap.

'The operation is quite a success, and Rajah's walk already shows signs that the pain is less.'
*Daily News, 3 May 1927*

Anaesthetic practice in the 1970s
'Seventy-two mammals and 38 birds were examined under general anaesthesia during 1973. Ketamine hydrochloride (Vetalar, Parke

Trimming an elephant's feet, 1919

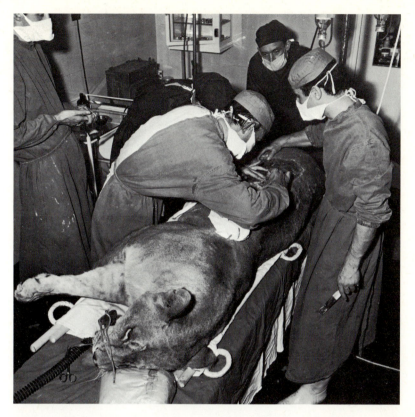

The Veterinary Surgeon operates on a lioness in the Society's
well-equipped Animal Hospital opened in 1956

Davis), is now in routine use for chemical restraint in the wild cats
and primates and is being tried in wallabies. Our experience with
ketamine hydrochloride indicates that it has considerable advantages
over phencyclidine hydrochloride (Sernylan, Parke Davis); onset of
"sedation" is rapid, taking only 5 to 8 minutes following intramuscular
injection, the laryngeal and pharyngeal reflexes are preserved and
recovery is complete in about 6 to 8 hours, compared with up to 36
hours with phencyclidine hydrochloride ...'
*Scientific Report, 1971–3*

Dermatitis in a rhino at Whipsnade
'Two three-year-old White rhinoceroses (*Diceros simus*) developed a
severe exudative dermatitis during the winter of 1970/1. The lesions
began as raised papules which ultimately became erosions some 1–2 cm

in diameter. These occupied the skin surface of the dorsal half of the body, and also the whole of the head and neck. Many of the erosions coalesced to form extensive irregular lesions over which a quantity of encrusted exudate formed ... Treatment was carried out by spraying a suspension of 0.5 g thiabendazole and 1.0 g of oxytetracycline in 500 ml of cod liver oil on to the lesions every other day for a month. It is very important to ensure that if rhinoceroses do not have access to water for long periods the epidermal layers of their skins remain intact. Application of vegetable or cod liver oils are suitable for this purpose.'

*Scientific Report, 1971–3*

# [4]

# Science and Zoo

'When science is *merely* subsidiary to practical ends it
leads you into blind alleys. Look at the Babylonians
and Egyptians. The scientist should always start from
pure curiosity. Then if he happens to find that his
goose lays golden eggs, he can, of course, present the
gold to the Bank and avert a national crisis. But that is
only by the way. During the War, now, the Zoo became
highly practical. While private individuals were planting
out their tennis lawns with mangolds, the Zoo not only
did similar vegetable gardening, but lunched the troops
in its restaurant, held exhibitions to demonstrate the
dangers of blowflies and horseflies, invented new ways
to deal with manure and refuse, gave an exhibition of
intensive poultry farming, bought two hundred and
four young pigs to rear and sell for bacon, held another
exhibition to demonstrate the wickedness of rats and
mice and to publicize the methods of their destruction,
and—most noble of all—sacrificed a number of their

show animals for food. After the War, naturally, they had to restock.

'Q.: Now that's what I want to know. How do they *get* these animals?

'A.: Oh, that's a long story. A few animals arrive by accident, especially in freights of bananas from South America; snakes, bird-eating spiders, even opossums. These reach the Zoo from markets or greengrocers who discover them. Many animals are bought from dealers in the ports, in Liverpool, Marseilles or Hamburg.'
*Zoo, by Louis MacNeice, 1938*

# [4]
# Science and Zoo

## Research and publications

'The advancement of zoology and animal physiology ...'. This was the first part of the Society's objectives as stated in 1826 and it still applies today. While the Zoological Gardens were being established in Regent's Park, the scientists in the Society were already holding scientific meetings for discussion and carrying out research, mainly anatomical, on a wide range of animals. The results of this work have been published in a long series of publications, known as the *Proceedings* (from 1830) and *Transactions* (from 1835) of the Zoological Society. These journals were illustrated with some of the finest anatomical drawings and they form one of the principal sources of our knowledge of comparative anatomy, particularly of mammals and birds. An outstanding nineteenth-century figure in this field was Sir Richard Owen, who in addition to his professorial duties, undertook a vast amount of work on the anatomy of animals, and finished his career as Superintendent of the Natural History Department of the British Museum; in fact he organized the removal of the nation's natural history collections from Bloomsbury to the present Natural History Museum in South Kensington.

Owen's scientific output was enormous, and much of his original work was published by the Zoological Society. During the early years of the Society's history he produced original papers on the anatomy of such familiar animals as the orang-utan, chimpanzee, gorilla, giraffe, cheetah, tapir, seal, beaver, echidna, flamingo, kiwi and gannet.

The Society now runs two research institutes, the Nuffield Institute of Comparative Medicine (opened in 1965) and the Wellcome Institute of Comparative Physiology (opened in 1964), each with highly qualified permanent and visiting scientific workers.

Nature and status of the Society
'Our Society is a scientific and educational institution which was incorporated in 1829 for the sole purpose of advancing zoology and animal physiology, and of introducing "new and curious subjects of the animal kingdom". This object, as laid down in our Royal Charters,

A kiwi (*Apteryx Australis*), from a drawing by Richard Owen
and W. Scharf in *Transactions*, *1849*

strictly confines the activities the Society can undertake and its rights
in law. The Society can advance zoology only by adding to the store
of zoological knowledge, or by helping, through its educational
activities, to spread that knowledge.'
*Annual Report*, *1957*

An early anatomical exercise
'ROYAL OSTRICH. One of the fine ostriches, recently brought to
England by Major Denham, died last week, in the Royal Menagerie,
at Windsor. The bird was in the finest plumage and condition; and
to render the skin and internal structure of so interesting a specimen
available to the purposes of science, His Majesty signified his pleasure
that it should be presented to the Zoological Society. The skin has
been accordingly preserved; and, with preparations of several of the
internal parts, will be placed in the Museum in Bruton Street. On
Friday the body of the ostrich was dissected, in the presence of a
number of distinguished professors and lovers of science, when a
most interesting demonstration of its anatomy took place. Large
pieces of wood, iron nails, eggs, &c., were found in the stomach.

The cause of its death was pronounced to be obesity. After the operation the gentlemen partook of a portion of the flesh, which was declared to be excellent, and much resembling beef. The Court of Aldermen were not invited.'
*Press Cutting, 27 August 1827*

Richard Owen dissects a giraffe
'Owen now [1838] began gradually to relinquish his medical practice, in order to devote the whole of his time to scientific research. Meanwhile, he never neglected the opportunities which occurred of dissecting the animals which died at the Zoological Society's Gardens; and these opportunities were naturally of frequent occurrence at a time when the habits and mode of life of the animals were but imperfectly understood. Constant reference is made in the diaries to these dissections. The carcases of such animals as Owen could obtain from menageries and other sources he not unfrequently dissected at home. Those dying at the Zoological Gardens were dissected there. On 29 January we read in his wife's journal:
'"Today Richard cut up the giraffe which died at the Zoological Gardens. Afterwards he went to the Royal Institution to dissect a snake."'
*The Life of Richard Owen, by Richard Owen, 1894*

Charles Darwin and the Zoological Society
'It was ordered, at the request of C. Darwin, Esq., Corr. Memb. of the Society [elected a Fellow of the Society in 1831], that that gentleman be allowed access to any written records kept at the Gardens, containing facts of interest to the zoologist.'
*Minutes, 3 October 1838*

The Society disposes of its Museum
'Read the following Report from the Committee appointed 19 Dec. 1849 to consider Mr Bowerbank's proposition for the transfer of the Museum to Government, dated 28 June.
  'That it is the opinion of this Committee that it is desirable for the general advantage of science, as well as for the pecuniary position and increased utility of the Zoological Society, that the specimens in their Museum be offered to the Government for a fair and sufficient equivalent.
  'And the Committee beg to recommend to the Council that a

[111]

treaty for this purpose be suggested to Her Majesty's Government ...

'Because the consolidation of the Zoological Department of the Society's Museum with the Zoological Department of the British Museum and of the Anatomical Department with the Hunterian Museum will greatly facilitate the researches of students in natural history ...' [Most of the collection went to the British Museum (Natural History), an institution which still has first call on the dead specimens after post-mortem.]

*Minutes, 3 July 1850*

In 1865 Professor T.H.Huxley became chairman of a committee 'to consider the mode by which the animals dying in the Gardens may be disposed of with most benefit to Zoological Science'. They recommended post-mortem examinations, and these have been carried out ever since.

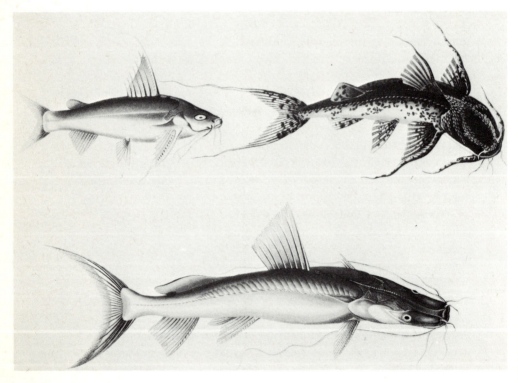

Catfishes, from *Transactions, 1841*

Letters from Charles Darwin to A.D. Bartlett

'August 24, 1860

Dear Sir, I have directed a copy of my *Origin of Species* to be sent to your address to the Zoo rooms in Hanover Square, and I hope that you will do me the favour to accept it. If you will read article on Hybridism, at page 264, you will see why I am anxious about the embryos in eggs from first crosses. I was very glad to see a donkey with a wild ass in the Gardens, for I infer from this that you intend rearing a hybrid; if so I hope that you will look carefully for stripes on the *shoulder and legs in the foal*: you will see why I am so anxious on this head, if you will read the little discussion in the *Origin* from p. 163–167.

'I will let you hear about the Moscow rabbits after I have heard from the young lady who brought them, whether she consents to their being sent to the Gardens. If you should hear from Hunt anything about the record of the gestation of the *Canidae*, or about the parents of hybrid jackals, perhaps you will be so kind as to inform me.

'I was much interested by the facts you kindly communicated to me, and remain, dear sir, yours very faithfully, Charles Darwin.

'May 21, 1861

Dear Sir, The bearer will deliver three rabbits (if none dead on voyage) from Madeira. Will you take charge of them for me, and show this note to Mr Sclater? They are zoologically very interesting, for they have run wild on a little island of Porto Santo since the year 1420; and judging from two dead ones seen by me, they have become greatly reduced in size and modified in colour and in their skeletons. I want much to see them alive, and to try whether they will cross freely with common rabbits. I am going immediately to leave home for two months. Would there be any objection to your keeping them for some time and matching them with some other breed; or if you think fit, first try and get some purely bred?

'I may perhaps be mistaken, but I was very much surprised at many of the characters of the two dead specimens which I saw.

'If any one should die, I should like its skeleton. Pray forgive me troubling you, but I know not what to do with them at present.

'If worth consideration, I would of course pay for their keep. In haste, dear sir yours very faithfully, Charles Darwin.'

[113]

'With reference to the above rabbits, Darwin wrote—"The two little Porto Santo rabbits, whilst alive in the Zoological Gardens, had a remarkably different appearance from the common kind. They were extraordinarily wild and active, so that many persons exclaimed on seeing them that they were more like large rats than rabbits. They were nocturnal to an unusual degree in their habits, and their wildness was never in the least subdued; so that the Superintendent, Mr Bartlett, assured me that he never had a wilder animal under his charge. This is a singular fact, considering that they are descended from a domesticated breed. Lastly, and this is a highly remarkable fact, Mr Bartlett could never succeed in getting these two rabbits, which were both males, to associate or breed with the females of several breeds which were repeatedly placed with them."

'The two rabbits above-mentioned were deposited in the Society's Gardens, 21 May 1861, and entered as two females, but Mr Darwin says they were males.'

'January 30, 1865
My Dear Sir, You have two rabbits of mine from Porto Santo. Will you be so good as to have one of them killed, taking great care that the skull and vertebrae are not broken, and sent as soon as you can, addressed: C. Darwin, Esq., *Care of* Down Postman, Bromley, Kent. Per rail.

'I shall be very much obliged if you will inform me whether you have got young from these rabbits with the females of other breeds?

'I want to beg one other favour; I want to examine under the microscope the tipped feathers of *Gallus sonneratii*. Could you send me one or two? Believe me, my dear sir, yours very faithfully, Charles Darwin.'
*Life among Wild Beasts in the 'Zoo', by A.D. Bartlett, 1900*

A newly discovered deer goes to the British Museum
'The Secretary also reported the arrival of a skin and skeleton of *Elaphurus davidianus*, being those of one of the animals presented to the Society at Peking by M. de Bellone, which had died before it could be transmitted home.

'It was agreed that the skeleton of this animal should be presented to the Museum of the Royal College of Surgeons, and the skin to the British Museum.'
*Minutes, 21 October 1868*

[114]

Spectacled cayman, so-called because of the markings round its
eyes, from *Transactions, 1867*

Père David's Deer (*Elaphurus davidianus*) has never been found in
the wild. It was discovered, about 1865, when Père Armand David,
a French missionary and naturalist, looked over the wall of the
Imperial Park of Hai-tzu, a few miles south of Peking, and saw a
herd of about 120 of them. By the turn of the century this herd had
been exterminated, but the Duke of Bedford, then President of the
Zoological Society, had previously obtained living specimens which
he kept at Woburn Park in Bedfordshire. From there, breeding stocks
have been distributed to many parts of the world, and in 1957 the
Zoological Society sent some back to China where they now live in
the Peking Zoo.

A request from Francis Galton
'A communication was read from Francis Galton Esq. [(1822–1911)
cousin of Charles Darwin and founder of the science of eugenics],
requesting permission to make certain scientific experiments in

breeding rabbits in the Society's Gardens, whereupon it was agreed that the Secretary be authorized to give Mr Galton the necessary facilities for this purpose.'
*Minutes, 15 December 1869*

Plans for more African fauna
'The Secretary having called the attention of the Council to the two Livingstone expeditions about to be sent out by the Royal Geographical Society into unexplored parts of tropical Africa, the following resolution was agreed to:

'The Council beg leave to call the attention of the Council of the Royal Geographical Society to the importance of investigating the Zoology of the countries about to be traversed by the Livingstone expeditions, and to the desirability of obtaining Zoological specimens in these countries so far as this can be done consistently with the main objects of the expeditions, and the Council of the Zoological Society are willing to contribute towards any additional expenditure, as regards outfit or otherwise, which may thus be rendered necessary, to an amount not exceeding £100.'
*Minutes, 20 November 1872*

At the death of Charles Darwin
'It was proposed by Professor Newton, seconded by Professor Mivart, and carried unanimously:

'That this Council desires to record its deep sense of the extraordinary value of the scientific labours of the late Mr Charles Darwin, a Fellow of this Society, and that a copy of this resolution be communicated to Mrs Darwin as an expression of sympathy with her and the rest of her family at the irreparable loss which they have sustained by his death.'
*Minutes, 3 May 1882*

Scientific Meetings
These meetings form an important part of the Society. The first meeting of what was then known as the Committee of Science and Correspondence took place on 9 November 1830, when Richard Owen read the first part of his paper on the 'Anatomy of the Orangutan'.

The chief members of this committee are shown in a contemporary cartoon from *Punch*: 'Sir Richard Owen (1804–92), the great nineteenth-century anatomist, is sitting in front of Mr Punch and holding a Kiwi (*Apteryx*), on which he had written the original monograph in the Society's *Transactions* in the 1830s and 1840s.

Sir William Henry Flower (1831–99) was Director of the British Museum (Natural History) (1884–98), and President of the Zoological Society (1879 until his death).

Thomas Henry Huxley (1825–95)—known as Darwin's Bulldog—because he championed the theory laid down in the *Origin of Species*—was one of the most influential scientists of the nineteenth century.

Sir Edwin Ray Lankester (1847–1929) succeeded Sir William Flower as Director of the British Museum (Natural History), and Philip Lutley Sclater (1829–1913), a pioneer in the study of zoogeography, was Secretary of the Zoological Society of London (1859–1902).'

The discovery of a new African mammal
'It is many years since the Meeting Room of the Zoological Society was so crowded as it was last night. The room was so full that it was difficult to get near the table on which two skulls of the much-discussed okapi—to give the creature its native name—were exhibited. Their molar teeth were so evidently those of a ruminant (not of a horse),

[117]

that there could be no question about them. But, if confirmation were needed it was there, in the absence of incisor teeth from the upper jaw, and their replacement by a hard fleshy pad, the dried remains of which still clothed the bones. When the Chairman (Professor G.B. Howes, F.R.S., Vice President) entered the room there was not a vacant seat.

'Mr Oldfield Thomas, F.R.S., on behalf of Professor Ray Lankester, read a short paper on the new African mammal. Before doing so Mr Thomas unrolled the skin (which, with the skulls, had only just been

The Okapi, from the original drawing by its discoverer,
Sir Harry Johnston, K.C.B.

received at the Museum) ... But the form was so different from that of the giraffe that, though it belonged to the same family, it was necessary to found a distinct genus for it, which Professor Lankester proposed to call *Okapia*, from the native name okapi. The name of the animal would, therefore, be *Okapia Johnstoni*.

'Sir Harry Johnston [explorer, naturalist and colonial administrator], who was received with applause, said that the first person to draw attention to this new mammal was undoubtedly Stanley, who learnt from the dwarfs the existence of a horse-like animal in the depths of the forest. He himself had questioned them about the animal, which they certainly believed to be a horse (in the technical sense), for when asked what it was like, they pointed to a young tame zebra which he had with him. He spent several days in the Semliki Forest, searching for the okapi, and once they saw it, but never came up with it. For a long time he tried to purchase a skin, but could only get pieces of the gaudily coloured parts on the flanks, all the dark body part being neglected. Little could be ascertained of the habits of the animal, beyond the fact that it went about in pairs—a male and a female together—and was only to be found in the deepest recesses of the forest, which lay to the west and south of the Albert Nyanza ...

'Some discussion ensued, in the course of which warm testimony was borne to Sir Harry's exertions in the cause of zoological science.'
*Standard*, *19 June 1901*

The great *Tarsius* debate, 1919
An up-and-coming young anatomist challenged the established thinking ... 'Not long afterwards, in 1919, there took place in the old Meeting Room of the Zoological Society, now part of our Library, a discussion on the "Zoological position and affinities of *Tarsius*" (Woodward *et al.*, 1919). This discussion was a milestone in the history of primate studies and was instigated by Wood Jones himself. Many of the "heavy-weights" of the period participated.

'Smith Woodward, the British Museum's leading palaeontologist, spoke first, and was followed by Elliot Smith, who was perhaps unnecessarily scathing in his remarks, although the printed record does not indicate that he ever referred to Wood Jones by name. Then came J.P.Hill, whose criticisms were levelled on embryological grounds. Wood Jones "batted" fourth, and no doubt out of respect to those of his elders and betters who had already spoken, put his case with great moderation, but without qualifying his view that

*Tarsius* was more closely related to man than the latter was to the anthropoid apes.

'Mr R.I.Pocock, the distinguished zoologist, then the Society's Curator of Mammals, spoke next, but again in opposition to Wood Jones. He was followed by Chalmers Mitchell, Secretary of the Zoological Society, who thanked Wood Jones for initiating the debate, at the same time remarking that Wood Jones had been "more reticent" in the discussion than he usually was in addresses to more popular audiences, where "he attacked Darwinian evolutionists and Huxley in particular". The discussion was summed up by Professor E.W. MacBride who again added to injury by remarking that Wood Jones had "rather shrunk during the discussion" from a view "to which he had liberally committed himself in recent books published by him", namely that *Tarsius* and man agreed in retaining some primitive characteristics which monkeys and apes had lost ...

'It must have been a remarkable occasion because of the polemics. And it is equally remarkable because, in retrospect, Wood Jones was insisting that *Tarsius* was what all today accept it to be—a true primate —and not just some aberrant lemur.'
*Address by Lord Zuckerman at the Society's symposium on 'The Concepts of Human Evolution', 1972*

Scientific publications
The *Journal of Zoology*, formerly the *Proceedings*, is now published monthly. It contains original scientific papers covering a wide field of zoology, many of which have been read at the Scientific Meetings of the Society. Volumes 175, 176 and 177 appeared in 1975.

Apart from the *Transactions*, mentioned below, the Society also publishes the papers read at its *Symposia*, and the *Zoological Record*, an annual bibliography of the literature of zoology, now in its 109th volume.

In the field of zoo management, the Society has, since 1959, published the *International Zoo Yearbook*.

'An odd feature of modern civilization, although we are so accustomed to it as to take it for granted, is that scientific investigators not only are seldom paid for writing the memoirs [scientific papers] in which they describe their scientific work, but often have great difficulty in getting them published. Our *Scientific Proceedings*, published in unbroken annual series since 1830, and our *Scientific Transactions*, published at intervals since 1835, have been the means of making known a vast body of original research. There are few of the great Zoological writers of the last century whose names do not appear in our lists of authors. But the successive Committees of Publications have judged each paper offered on its merits rather than on its authorship, and the Society has thus been able to give an opportunity to many young zoologists.'

*Annual Report, 1929*

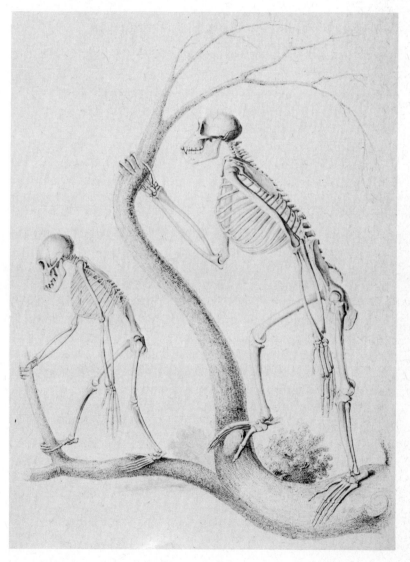

An engraving of chimpanzee skeletons, from a drawing by Richard Owen. *Transactions, 1835*

Every paper submitted for publication is critically assessed, and some are rejected even when written by a senior member of the British Museum staff ... 'Read a letter from Dr Gray complaining of the Publication Committee having returned to him a communication addressed to them, as not being "upon a suitable subject for the Society's Scientific Meetings". In reply to this it was agreed to point out to Dr Gray, that the arrangements of the Scientific Meetings were entrusted by the By-laws, to the Publication Committee, and that the Council, although they regretted that Dr Gray should have been annoyed by the decision of the Committee, did not think it expedient to interfere with it.'
*Minutes, 15 March 1871*

An Institute of Comparative Medicine at Regent's Park
'In April the Council was happy to announce that the Trustees of the Nuffield Foundation had agreed to grant the Society £100,000 to found an Institute of Comparative Medicine ...

'Almost from the day that the Regent's Park Gardens were founded in 1826 arrangements were made to provide veterinary care for the animals in the Society's collection, and to conduct pathological observations on those which died. In 1903 a full-time pathologist was appointed to the staff, but it was not until 1951 that he was joined by a resident veterinary surgeon, the Society until then having relied on the expert advice which could always be called on from the Royal Veterinary College, the London School of Hygiene and Tropical Medicine, and from various interested members of the medical profession. From its inception the Society had also provided research workers in different institutions with material for the study of isolated problems in comparative anatomy, comparative pathology, comparative haematology and comparative parasitology, and had sometimes found "bench space" for the occasional student.

'Unfortunately the laboratory facilities of the Society have been very restricted, and have never been sufficient to permit of any long-continued and exhaustive study in any aspect of comparative medicine; nor has the Society been able to employ a research staff to exploit the opportunities which daily present themselves for studies in comparative medicine.

'All this will be transformed as a result of the existence of an Institute of Comparative Medicine.'
*Annual Report, 1960*

Apart from the scientific work in its own laboratories, the Society
has always helped other institutions by supplying material gratis for
research purposes. Some examples in recent years include: feather
lice to the British Museum, egg shells and feathers for pigment
investigation to Sheffield University, optical pigments from the
Giant Panda eye to Sussex University and heads of psittacine birds
to the Royal Veterinary College.

A drawing by Edward Lear of the Pretty Face Wallaby of New
South Wales and Queensland. Note Lear's whimsical method
of illustrating the dentition. *Transactions, 1835*

## Education and conservation

The Society has always been involved in zoological education at different levels—making provision for children, keepers, students and even teachers.

A school party
'A letter was read from Mrs Robinson, dated 24 inst, containing a request that the children of the School of Christ's Hospital might be permitted to visit the Society's Gardens, permission for which was granted, with the understanding that at each visit the number of boys so admitted should not exceed a hundred.'
*Minutes, 26 April 1832*

And in 1850, but with strings attached ... 'The Secretary having read a letter from Mr Crew, Secretary of the Royal Caledonian Asylum requesting admission to the Gardens for the children on Thursdays, was authorized to accede to Mr Crew's request, on condition of the band of the Asylum being permitted by the Directors to perform in the Gardens when required.' [The Royal Caledonian Asylum in the Caledonian Road was established in 1815 'for the relief of the children of soldiers, sailors and mariners, natives of Scotland, who have died or been disabled in the service of their country; and the children of indigent Scotch parents residing in London, not entitled to parochial relief'.]
*Minutes, 16 October 1850*

Public Lectures in the nineteenth century
'ZOOLOGICAL LECTURES. The Council have determined that the Davis Fund for the present year shall again be devoted to popular lectures on subjects connected with the living collection in the Society's menagerie. These are given in the Lecture-Room in the Society's Gardens, on Thursdays, at 5, and have been arranged as follows:

| | Date | Subject | Lecturer |
|---|---|---|---|
| 1 | Thursday, April 27 | The Society's Gardens and their Inhabitants.......... | P. L. Sclater, Esq., F.R.S. |
| 2 | Thursday, May 4 | Rhinoceroses and Tapirs }<br>Horses and Zebras } | Professor Flower, F.R.S. |
| 3 | Thursday, May 11 | | |
| 4 | Thursday, May 18 | The Manatee............. | Dr J. Murie, F.Z.S. |
| 5 | Thursday, May 25 | Birds.................... | Professor Garrod, F.Z.S. |
| 6 | Thursday, June 1 | Bats.................... | Professor Mivart, F.R.S. |

| 7 | Thursday, June 8 | Homing Pigeons . . . . . . . . . . | W. B. Tegetmeier, Esq., F.Z.S. |
| 8 | Thursday, June 15 | Reptiles . . . . . . . . . . . . . . . . | Professor Garrod, F.Z.S. |
| 9 | Thursday, June 22 | The Beaver and its distribution . . . . . . . . . . . | J. W. Clark, Esq., F.Z.S. |
| 10 | Thursday, June 29 | The Zoological Station at Naples . . . . . . . . . . . . . . | Dr Carpenter, F.R.S. |

'The Lectures are free to Fellows of the Society and their friends, and to other visitors to the Gardens.'
*Annual Report, 1875*

Staff education
'Read a letter from Sir Chas. Lyall, F.Z.S., suggesting that a Library of Natural History Works, for the use of the keepers in the Society's Gardens should be provided; after some discussion, it was agreed that this suggestion should be adopted.'
*Minutes, 1 April 1868*

And now keepers' training is highly professional ... 'Of the eighteen members of the staff, at London and Whipsnade, who completed the course for the Ordinary Certificate in Zoo Animal Management, organized in conjunction with Paddington Technical College, seventeen were successful in the final examination; Messrs B. Blackburn, M. Gibbons, P. Hill and N. Virtue achieving distinction. All the eight members of staff who completed the Higher Certificate Course were successful in the final examination, Messrs M. Moore, L. Smith and P. Williams achieving distinction. Further courses for the Ordinary and Higher Certificates started in October.

'Throughout the year the Society has offered facilities for in-service training and experience for keeper staff from foreign zoos, including four from Nigeria, two from Copenhagen, one from Helsinki and one from Kuwait. Two students from Atlantic College in Wales spent a short period working in London Zoo as part of a special project.'
*Annual Report, 1973*

Zoology for young people
There is now an Education Department staffed by three qualified zoologists. During 1974 they lectured to about 56,000 children at Regent's Park and 4,000 at Whipsnade. Primary school children could learn about monkeys and apes, reptiles, or the Zoo and how it

works, while secondary school children had sessions on topics such as mammalian limbs, adaptations to feeding, conservation, or size and shape in animals. And there are ...

Christmas lectures for young people. In 1973 Dr Johns Sparks, of the BBC's Natural History Unit, spoke on 'Filming animals for television', and Professor J. L. Cloudsley-Thompson gave an illustrated talk on 'African animals'.

Activities of the Young Zoologists' Club '... were well supported and members visited Bristol Zoo and the Norfolk Wildlife Park at Great Witchingham. Zoo Quest competitions were held both at Regent's Park and Whipsnade Park during the summer holiday periods. Indoor meetings included talks by Mr Hugh Falkus and by members of the Society's staff.

'Three editions of *Zoo Magazine* were published giving accounts of the latest developments at Regent's Park and Whipsnade, and a variety of articles on zoological topics.'
*Annual Report, 1974*


And to teach the teachers
'The Council, in co-operation with the Education Committee of the London County Council, was able to institute a scheme for the instruction of school teachers, so as to make the visits of school children to the Gardens more interesting and useful. One course took place in the autumn of 1910, and was followed by two courses early in 1911. The Secretary gave an inaugural lecture at which over 300 teachers were present. The courses were conducted by Mr J. L. Bonhote, F.Z.S., and each course provided for 150 teachers, who attended three lectures with lantern demonstrations in the new Meeting Hall, whilst they were given practical demonstrations in the Gardens in sets of twenty-five. Very great interest was taken by the teachers, and it is expected that the courses will be continued next autumn and winter on a large scale.'
*Annual Report, 1910*


Letters from the public arrive in a constant stream
'Sir, You will much oblige me by giving me information upon a subject, which from your position you will be well able to do. I presume that you have among the collection of animals at the Gardens "the Hare". I am anxious to know in reference to this animal whether it "chews the cud". In *The Times* newspaper of today, there is an

assertion made by Bishop Colenso, founded on the authority of Professor Owen, that it does *not* chew the cud. In the eleventh chapter of Leviticus, sixth verse, it is stated that the Jews were forbidden to use it as an article of food because it does chew the cud.

'Explanations are given in books I have referred to, stating that from a peculiar movement of the mouth it appears to do so,—but it does not. Cowper the poet describes one of his own, which during the day, when in his garden, "either slept or chewed the cud till the evening". I am giving you trouble, I fear, in thus writing to you, but *actual observation* surely is the best means of judging.

'Is it in appearance only, or is it a fact? The Bible says it is the fact, and I entirely believe it. But naturalists deny it. By giving me the above information I have requested, you will much oblige me, etc., etc., H. Battiscombe.'

'Zoo April 3, 1863.
Dear Sir, In reply to your letter respecting the Hare, I beg to say that I have several living in the collection, having for some years carefully studied these animals in every stage of their existence, in order if possible to obtain a cross between this animal and the rabbit, to which it is nearly allied. I have in consequence become well acquainted with its habits and structure, both external and internal; my frequent examinations of the stomach and intestines have convinced me that these animals have not the power to, and consequently do not "*chew the cud*".

'The structure of the stomach of all ruminating animals is remarkable, and well known to comparative anatomists; and this peculiar structure does not exist in any of the order *Rodentia* to which the Hare belongs.

'The animals possess very fleshy lips, and the muscles of the mouth are largely developed; by these means the parts are moved with great ease and kept in almost constant motion, and thus, when noticed by persons whose knowledge of the subject is limited, might easily lead them to believe that the animal was chewing, and this has doubtless led to the mistake made by the early writers. Believe me to be, Dear Sir, Yours faithfully, A. D. Bartlett.
Rev. H. Battiscombe, 18 Lee Park, Blackheath.'
*Life among Wild Beasts in the 'Zoo', by A. D. Bartlett, 1900*

'To the Reptile House Keeper—Dear Sir, We would be most grateful if you could help us in any way, I have a tortoise, I bought her over two years ago, she was very tiny, but has grown a lot, she has never hibernated, and we kept her in the living room, she walked all over the room, about a fortnight ago we bought a puppy, she kept going to the tortoise, and so she would not be able to torment her, my Mother put the tortoise in her box in which she sleeps at night, and put the box on top of some cushions on a chair, I think the tortoise must have started climbing out of her box, because we heard a crash, I rushed to pick her up, her head was in her shell, and her front legs were waving about furiously.

'I nursed her for a long time and she calmed down, there was a spot of blood on her nose, her eyes were closed and very swollen, it looked as if the front of her shell had pressed in to the top of her head, this happened a week last Monday, I took her to a veterinary surgeon, but was told they did not know a lot about tortoises, she was given an injection, and some powder called Terramycin, to put in her water, but she won't drink it, she has been eating up till yesterday, although she would not eat anything for the first three days after she fell, she is lively, and walks about, but her eyes are not properly open, her left one is still closed, and her right eye looks strange ...
Yours Respectfully ...' 1972

'Dear Sir, You being an expert on birds I wonder if you can help us! A month ago we purchased a Red Macaw, since the day we had him he is vomiting all his food. He starts by jerking his head backwards and forwards and flapping his wings, and so bringing up what he's eaten. We have had two vets to him, one wasn't too sure what was wrong with him and advised us to get in touch with a bird sanctuary, which we did! They said he could have mating instincts, the other vet said he was suffering from acute indigestion, but with all the treatment he is still the same. He isn't a very big eater and not too keen on fruit, except a little orange or banana. He looks healthy and is lively, but its just this problem with his digestion, if you could advise us in any way, we would be most grateful to you. By the way he's two years old! Yours faithfully ...' 1971

Extract from letter, October 1969 ... 'I have no idea how much it costs to run a parrot ...'

August 1974 ... 'My cockatoo escaped last night. Could you tell me in which direction he will fly ...'

and telephone calls from gullible members of the public who have been primed to ask for Mr C. Lyon, Miss Ann Teater, Mr Terry Pin, Mr Albert Ross, Mr G. Raff, Mr Don Key, Mr R. Madillo, Mr L. E. Fant, Miss Sally Mander or Mr Jim Panzi; some of these have even come from New York.

Conservation

The conservation movement is now an active force in all parts of the world, but even in the last century the Zoological Society of London had started to encourage the protection of endangered animals in Britain, such as the Great Skua ...

'The Council have agreed, in recognition of the effective protection accorded for sixty years to the Great Skua (*Stercorarius catarrhactes*) at two of its three British breeding-stations—namely, in the island of Unst by the late Dr Laurence Edmonston and other members of the same family, and in the island of Foula by the late Dr Scott, of Melby, and his son Mr Robert T. C. Scott—to award the Silver Medal of the Society to Mrs Edmonston, of Buness House, as representative of that family, and to Robert T. C. Scott, Esq., of Melby.

'In departing from the usual practice of awarding the Society's medals for services personally rendered to the Society the Council have been influenced by the consideration that the extermination of various species of animals, which has been going on with increasing rapidity in so many parts of the world, will in a few years form a serious detriment to the progress of zoological science. The total extinction with which several forms of animal life are inevitably threatened in several of the British Colonies will ever be deeply regretted by future investigators, and steps taken for their protection should accordingly be worthy of reward.'
*Annual Report, 1890*

Of animals in other parts of the world

'Read a letter from The Earl of Onslow on the subject of the preservation of the native birds of New Zealand, whereupon the following resolutions were agreed to:

'That the Council of this Society have learnt with great satisfaction

the steps that were proposed to be taken by The Earl of Onslow, when
Governor of New Zealand, and by the Houses of General Assembly,
for the preservation of the native birds of New Zealand, by reserving
certain small islands suitable for the purpose, and by affording the
birds special protection on these islands.

'That the Council much regret to hear that difficulties have been
encountered in carrying out this plan as regards one of these islands
(Little Barrier Island), and trust that the Government of New
Zealand may be induced to take the necessary steps to overcome these
difficulties, and to carry out this excellent scheme in its entirety.

'The Council venture to suggest that, besides the native birds to
be protected in these reserves, shelter should also be afforded to the
remarkable Saurian, the Hatteria or Tuatara Lizard, which is at
present restricted to some small islands on the north coast of New
Zealand in the Bay of Plenty.

'That copies of these resolutions be communicated to The Earl of
Onslow, and to His Excellency, The Earl of Glasgow, the present
Governor of New Zealand.'
*Minutes, 1 February 1893*

And of the Osprey
'Professor Newton then called attention to the propriety of recognizing
the services of those that have afforded and are affording protection
to the Osprey in Scotland and moved: That the Society's Silver Medal
be presented to Donald Cameron, Esq. of Lochiel, and John Peter
Grant, Esq. of Rothiemurchus for their services in protecting the
Osprey in Scotland. This was agreed to.'
*Minutes, 15 March 1893*

'A letter having been read from the Foreign Office asking the Society
to entertain at the Gardens delegates representing the powers with
possessions in Africa, now in conference on the question of affording
protection to the elephant and rhinoceros, the Secretary stated that,
as the matter was urgent, he had sent the delegates cards of honorary
admission to the Gardens, and had arranged that they should be
invited to tea in the Fellows' Pavilion next day. This was approved
of, and it was agreed that the entertainment should be at the expense
of the Society, and that members of Council who were able to be
present should join the party.'
*Minutes, 20 May 1914*

Today the Society continues to support conservation and to honour those who write and broadcast about it. Recent recipients of the Society's Silver Medal include:

1965: David Attenborough, for his wide influence, particularly with young people, in the field of public education both through television programmes and through books.

1968: James Fisher, in recognition of his contribution to the understanding of zoology and to public appreciation of the importance of conservation.

The obverse and reverse sides of the Society's Silver Medal

Captive breeding helps to conserve endangered species
'Two orang-utans were born in the Michael Sobell Pavilions for Apes and Monkeys, one to the female "Bulu", who was born at Regent's Park in 1961. Since 1967, when the group of nine orang-utans arrived as a gift from the Government of Hong Kong, five young have been successfully reared, and we can now dispose of some of the animals while still maintaining the breeding potential of the group. One pair has been sent to Vienna Zoo to help establish a group, and another animal has been deposited with Twycross Zoo to make up a breeding pair. Provided the stock are transferred only to establishments which can house and care for them properly, breeding should continue and there should eventually be no further need for animals caught in the wild.'
*Annual Report, 1974*

[131]

Cheetahs that have successfully bred in the
parklands of Whipsnade

# [5]

# Keeping Animals and Visitors apart

'"These Mappin Terraces at the Zoological Gardens are a great improvement on the old-style of wild-beast cage," said Mrs James Gurtleberry, putting down an illustrated paper; "they give one the illusion of seeing the animals in their natural surroundings. I wonder how much of the illusion is passed on to the animals?"

'"That would depend on the animal," said her niece; "a jungle-fowl, for instance, would no doubt think its lawful jungle surroundings were faithfully reproduced if you gave it a sufficiency of wives, a goodly variety of seed food and ants' eggs, a commodious bank of loose earth to dust itself in, a convenient roosting tree, and a rival or two to make matters interesting. Of course there ought to be jungle cats and birds of prey and other agencies of sudden death to add to the illusion of liberty, but the bird's own imagination is capable of inventing those—look how a domestic fowl will squawk an alarm note if a rook or a wood-pigeon passes over its run when it has chickens."'

*The Toys of Peace, by H.H.Munro, 1919*

A view of the Camels' House and Clock Tower from a lithograph of 1835 by George Scharf. In the very early days llamas
were housed in this building.

# [5]
# Keeping Animals and Visitors apart

In the early days the Society was largely concerned with ensuring that the animals did not escape, and there were no qualms about using bars and wire mesh. Later in the nineteenth century there were attempts at creating animal enclosures that were not only functional but looked attractive to the human eye. It was not, however, until the present century that zoo design began, as Mrs James Gurtleberry said, to 'give one the illusion of seeing animals in their natural surroundings.' This movement gained momentum some forty years ago with the development of Whipsnade Park as a country zoo. At Whipsnade Park, opened in the spring of 1931, the emphasis is on open grassy paddocks with ditches rather than bricks separating man from animal, and here it is possible to keep animals in natural breeding groups. Whipsnade now has one of the most impressive records in the world for captive breeding.

At Regent's Park there has been continuous building activity since 1828. Much of the success in this field has been due to the imagination of the Society's architects. The great name in the early days was, of course, Decimus Burton, and it is gratifying to know that his Llamas' House (1828) and Giraffe House (1836) are still standing, and are, indeed, among the Greater London Council's Listed Structures.

Early in the twentieth century, J.J.Joass was responsible for designing the Mappin Terraces and the Aquarium, and in the 1930s Lubetkin designed the Penguin Pond and Gorilla House, both now Listed Structures.

A distinguished committee in 1839 considers tenders for the Monkey House ... 'Special meeting 1 June 1839. Present: Lord Braybrooke, V.P., in the Chair, C.Darwin Esq. [just back from the voyage of the *Beagle* in 1836], Jas. Whishaw, Esq., Wm. Ogilby, Esq., the Secretary, Sir F.Chantrey, Sir Geo. Clerk, Bt V.P., Capt. Bowles, V.P., Lord Seymour.

'The Secretary stated that ... tenders for the new Monkey House ...

The Aviary, from a lithograph of 1835 by George Scharf

having been received were read, viz.: Messrs Harvard and Nixon to
execute the work for £1385, Mr Crowe for £1298, Messrs Dicksons
and Co. for £1297 and Mr Windsland for £1239 ... It was resolved,
on the recommendation of the Finance Committee, that Mr
Winsland's tender be accepted.'
*Minutes, 1 June 1839*

The first Aquarium
'THE AQUATIC VIVARIUM. A living exhibition of the sea-bottom
and its odd inhabitants is such an absolute novelty, that we must
give our readers this week, at the risk of being charged with an undue
partiality for natural history, some account of the elegant aquatic
vivarium just opened to the public. On the borders of the flower-bed
in the Zoological Gardens, Regent's Park, has been constructed,
crystal-palace fashion, of glass and iron, a light airy building sixty by
twenty feet in area, containing around its transparent walls fourteen

Marine animals in the Aquatic Vivarium, 1858

six-feet tanks of plate glass. Eight tanks will, in the first instance, be devoted to living marine animals, and of these six are ready for exhibition. They enclose masses of rock, sand, gravel, corallines, sea-weed, and sea-water; and are abundantly stocked with crustacea, starfish, sea-eggs, actiniae, ascidians, shelled and shell-less molluscs, and fish of the genera *gasterosteus*, *labrus*, *crenilabrus*, *blennius*, *gobius*, and *cattus*. The whole are in a state of natural restlessness, now quiescent, now eating and being eaten.'
*Literary Gazette, 1853*

The Antelope House
In 1861 the Antelope House was built. A rather charming structure, it was demolished just over a hundred years later to make way for the new Elephant and Rhinoceros Pavilion. 'The Antelope House lately erected in the Gardens of the Zoological Society of London in Regent's Park was built for the Society by Messrs Lucas, the well-known

[137]

contractors, from the designs of Anthony Salvin, Esq., jun., at a cost of about £2,500. The building, of which we give herewith a view from the south side, is placed in the southern part of the Gardens, and stands at a right angle to the house containing the zebras, which was finished and opened to the public about two years ago. It measures 175 ft in length, by 22 ft in width, and is divided into fifteen commodious stalls, each of them communicating by sliding doors with those adjoining and with an open court in front. The fittings are substantially constructed of oak and wrought-iron bars. The whole of the open timberwork of the roof inside is stained and varnished, which adds greatly to the general effect of the interior. Ample means of ventilation have been secured by the dormer windows placed over each stall, and by ventilators fixed in the roof; and the whole edifice may be fairly said to be not only the most commodious and suitable building for animals as yet erected in the Society's Gardens, but also by no means deficient in architectural merits.'
*Press cutting, 1861*

The Antelope House. *Illustrated London News, 3 August 1861*

Explosion on the Canal at Regent's Park
'Early on the morning of 2 October, 1874 ... four barrels of gun-
powder exploded on board the barge *Tilbury* on the Regent's Canal,
just under the bridge at the end of Avenue Road. The shock was
severely felt along the canal bank, and fragments of the barge were
afterwards picked up by the Superintendent between his office and
the Elephant House. No serious damage was done, though it was
reported to the Council that "no house had entirely escaped injury".
Large quantities of glass were broken, and frames and sashes dis-
placed and shattered. The Western Aviary in the South Garden
suffered a good deal; some of the smaller birds made their way out,
but most of them were captured and brought back. According to the
*Annual Register*, "the explosion caused considerable commotion among
the animals, and their howling added considerably to the excitement
which the disaster caused in the neighbourhood". Fortunately, none
of the large animals was injured; and though they were greatly terrified,
they soon became quiet when the keepers arrived. In the following
year compensation was made by the Grand Junction Canal Company,
the owners of the barge.'
*The Zoological Society of London, by H. Scherren, 1905*

The Superintendent's report on the damage caused by the explosion:
'The injury done to the animals, themselves, I am glad to say, has
been trifling, and this I attribute principally to the utter darkness of
the morning, and the impossibility, in the awful confusion, to obtain
lights; two or three assistants, who are the only persons who sleep in
the Gardens, and I went into the different houses, and by calling and
speaking to the affrighted animals caused them to stop jumping and
rushing about ... A considerable number of birds escaped through
the openings in the roof of the Western Aviary. Many of them,
however, returned and allowed themselves to be caught and restored
to their former abode, others flew long distances and have been lost,
but these do not happen to be birds of much value, and can, therefore,
be easily replaced.
'For many days after the explosion I received letters from people
in the country (surrounding the Metropolis) informing me of strange
and beautiful birds that had appeared in their gardens, etc., and by
their kindness, several were recovered.
'It is impossible, at this moment, to estimate with any degree of
accuracy the amount of damage sustained by the Society, but after

carefully noting the repairs that have been necessary and what of
them remain to be carried out, I believe the cost will be about £300—
3 November, 1874.'
*Life among Wild Beasts in the 'Zoo', by A.D. Bartlett, 1900*

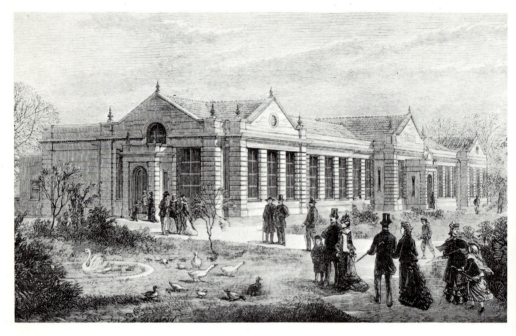

Visitors enjoy strolling outside the newly opened Lion House
in 1876

The Lion House, opened in 1876
(Removed in 1975 to make way for a newly designed complex for the
larger cats.)
'The new Lion House, when thus complete, will, it is believed, form
by far the largest and most perfect building for the accommodation
of the larger Carnivora ever erected. The total length of the main
building is 228 feet, exclusive of the porticoes; the width, up to the
front of the dens, 35 feet. The dens are fourteen in number, and
will accommodate, if necessary, as many pairs of animals, each animal
having a separate inside den. The larger dens measure 20 feet by 12
feet. The smaller are about 12 feet square. The height of the building
at the central elevation is 30 feet. At the back of the dens is a wide
passage extending the whole length of the building. From this passage
doors open into every inner den, and in this are fixed the chains and

pulleys for opening the sliding doors between the dens, so that the whole of the work connected with cleaning and management of the animals is effected from behind ...

'The present occupants of the Lion House consist of 6 Lions, 7 Tigers, 2 Jaguars, 2 Leopards, 3 Pumas, and a Clouded Tiger, altogether 21 in number. The only desideratum among the larger Felidae is the Ounce (*Felis uncia*) of the mountains of Central Asia, of which as yet no living specimen, it is believed, has ever been brought to this country.'

*Annual Report, 1875*

Owing to the rush to see the lions, visitors are advised to beware of pickpockets. *Daily Graphic, 2 September 1903*

The first Insect House in the world

'Although of late years many entomologists have been in the habit of rearing insects in captivity for the purpose of watching their transformations and of obtaining good specimens in each stage of their existence, nothing like a systematic attempt, so far as the Council knows, has yet been made to form a general collection of living insects for exhibition. As in former days with respect to reptiles and the lower marine animals, so in the present instance as regards its Insect House, the Society seems to be first in the field, and, so far as can be judged from the progress already made, to be likely to attain many interesting and instructive results.

'The building now used as an Insect House is constructed of iron and glass on three sides, with a brick back to it ... The cases containing the insects are arranged on stands all round the building, and also occupy two tables in the centre ...

'The cases on the south side (on each side of the entrance door) are mostly appropriated to the exhibition of the larger and finer species of silk-producing moths of the family Bombycidae.

'On the north side the smaller cases are devoted principally to the rarer and more noticeable butterflies and moths of Europe, such as the Swallow-tailed Butterfly (*Papilio machaon*), the Black-veined Butterfly (*Aporia crataegi*), the Purple Emperor (*Apatura iris*), and the Orange-tip (*Anthocharis cardamines*) among the former, and the Scarlet Tiger-moth (*Callimorpha dominula*) and Emperor Moth (*Saturnia carpini*) among the latter group ...'
*Annual Report, 1881*

And somebody to tend the insects
'To authorize the Secretary to engage Mr W. Watkins of 305 Goldhawk Road, Shepherd's Bush, to take charge of the Insectorium from 1 April, for six months at a salary of £15 per month.'
*Minutes, 16 March 1881*

A new Reptile House was built in 1883 to replace the first one built in 1849
(This building is now the Bird House.)
'The Council have to announce to the meeting that in consequence of the improved state of the Society's finances, they have determined that the erection of the new Reptile House, the necessity of which has been spoken of in several of the last reports, shall be commenced immediately, and that it is hoped that the building will be roofed in before Christmas.'
*Minutes, 16 April 1882*

# GUIDE-BOOK

## TO THE

# INSECT-HOUSE

## IN THE GARDENS OF

## THE ZOOLOGICAL SOCIETY OF LONDON.

THE INDIAN MOON-MOTH, Male.
(Half nat. size.)

LONDON:

PRINTED FOR THE SOCIETY,

AND

SOLD IN THEIR GARDENS IN THE REGENT'S PARK.

1881.

Price 2d.

An early proposal for a country zoo
'Read a letter from A. W. Hackett, Esq., F.Z.S. asking the Council to consider the advisability of establishing a supplementary Zoological Garden on the borders of Epping Forest.

'It was agreed to reply to Mr Hackett that his suggestion should receive due consideration.
*Minutes, 7 May 1884*

How the Mappin Terraces came to be built
'The Council has pleasure in announcing that it accepted the munificent offer made by Mr J. Newton Mappin, the head of the firm of Mappin & Webb, Ltd, as conveyed to the Secretary in the following letter:

158–162, Oxford Street, W—14 December, 1912.
Dear Dr Chalmers Mitchell, I have pleasure in asking you to inform the Council that I offer to present to the Society an installation for the panoramic display of wild animals as nearly as possible on the lines of the sketches and plans you showed me. I believe that such an

The Mappin Terraces

installation would be of great benefit to the community, and would be an important step in your successful efforts to make the London Zoological Gardens the best in the world from the point of view of the animals themselves and the visitors.

'If my offer be accepted it would be very agreeable to me if the Council were to arrange that it be associated with some special benefit to London shop assistants, as for instance, that they be admitted to the Gardens at the rate of sixpence instead of a shilling on an afternoon each week convenient to them.

'On hearing from you that the Council has accepted my proposal and undertakes to proceed with the installation of the panorama immediately, and to complete it within twelve months, I shall have much pleasure in defraying the cost of the work as it proceeds, and will arrange with my bankers for them to pay from time to time on certificates signed by you and the architects. I do not wish the cost of the installation to be made known, but you and Mr Joass know the limit to which I am prepared to go.

'I propose to leave the details to your experience so far as the arrangements for the animals go, and to Mr Joass with regard to architectural work; but I assume that the scheme will be carried out on the general lines of the sketches you showed me, except that I should prefer that money should not be spent on the tea pavilion until the best possible provision has been made for the animals. Yours very truly, (Signed) J. Newton Mappin.'

Plans for a new Aquarium
'The Secretary ... now thought it possible that a good aquarium might be constructed under the Mappin Terraces, and he desired permission to go further into the possibility of this, first by a visit to the New Aquarium at Berlin with Mr Boulenger, the Curator of Reptiles, and afterwards by the preparation of plans and estimates for submission to the Garden Committee and Council.'
*Minutes, 15 October 1913*

But no action until after the First World War
'The Secretary obtained leave to introduce discussion of a memorandum on an aquarium ...

'The memorandum proposed that the Society should proceed with the construction of a first-rate salt- and fresh-water aquarium under the Mappin Terraces. It stated that the Terraces had been originally

[145]

designed with the view of completing them with an aquarium ...
The present cost, corrected from estimates made at pre-war prices
was estimated provisionally at £50,000 ...

'The Secretary read a telegram from the President regretting his
inability to be present, and a letter in which he stated his opinion
that on the financial side the aquarium scheme seemed justified:
also a letter from the Duke of Rutland, asking the Council to consider
the possibility of the Aquarium ceasing to interest the public after a
few months, and hence doubting the wisdom of the Society under-
taking so large a scheme at present ...

'After a long discussion ... it was resolved unanimously: That the
Secretary's scheme for the establishment of a salt- and fresh-water
aquarium is approved in principle, and that he be authorized to take
such further steps as may be necessary to prepare detailed plans for
consideration ...'
*Minutes, 18 January 1922*

The Aquarium is opened in 1924
'LONDON FINDS ITS SOLE. Zoo Aquarium packed with visitors.
Deep sea monsters. The green gloom of the Zoo Aquarium was packed
with men, women and children all day long yesterday. Some of them
expressed their astonishment like this:

'"Marjorie, come here! Now, look at that thing behind the rock.
No, not the pink one, the black one waggling its whiskers. Of whom
does it remind you?"

'Through the darkness an awed voice replied promptly: "Auntie!"

'No doubt it did. Some of the monsters which live at the bottom
of the sea bear an uncanny resemblance to some of the monsters who
live on land. When the fat salamander lies, with a piece of meat in
his wide mouth, he looks exactly like a profiteer smoking a cigar. The
giant pike, with his protruding lower jaw, has a singular resemblance
to certain supercilious people.

'HIGH SPIRITS. A schoolboy discovered a remarkable likeness in
the axolotl, and he bent down to his brother and hissed, "Fish face!"

'The most popular tank in the Aquarium is the large sea-water
tank containing eels, whiting, and plaice. Women in particular were
fascinated by it. All of them presumably had met such fish on fish-
mongers' slabs and in the frying pan. Not one spectator had apparently
suspected a lemon sole of high spirits or a flounder of cumbersome
gaiety.

'"Look at them," cried a woman. "I never thought plaice behaved like that. Did you, Emma?"

'Emma replied that she would never have believed it had she not seen it with her own eyes. And it is difficult to believe that these funny flat fish that swim so quickly, turn somersaults, flop themselves into holes in the silver sand, and suddenly dash out and do a few back strokes under the nose of a four-foot conger eel are the same fish we have met so often in company with tartar sauce and lemon juice.

'FEEDING TIME. Henceforth Londoners will not be able to eat a well-grilled sole without at least a tinge of sentiment.

'Feeding time came as a surprise to yesterday's visitors. At three thirty a canful of minnows was emptied into the pike tank. There was a swirl, snap, snap, snap, and a gasp of dismay from the crowd. Shelled shrimps were fed to some fish, bullock's heart to others, chopped meat to the trout, and live crabs to the wrasse.

'Already most of the fish know their feeding time, and, prompt to the minute, face in one direction, waiting for the descent of their particular manna.'

*Daily Express, April 1924*

But there was a spot of bother with the glass ...

'"They're all out, Mum".

'A breathless night-watchman panted out these tidings as he stood on the doorstep of the Curator's House in the heart of the London Zoo.

'The hour was midnight.

'You may imagine what passed through the mind of Mrs D. Seth-Smith, wife of the Curator of Mammals and Birds, as the man tried to explain himself. He might be talking of wolves, elephants, tigers or merely hornets—unless he referred to a mass escape of the entire outfit.

'The unfortunate point was that Mr Seth-Smith was away from home and that his son—Mr D. W. Seth-Smith—had not got back from a social function.

'When the man was able to explain, his news was bad enough. The main sea-water tank in the new Aquarium had burst, 7,000 gallons specially imported from the Bay of Biscay had "Gone West", and a weird crowd of dog-fish, giant conger eels, skate, big turbot, large crabs, and poisonous "sting-rays" were fighting for breath in the main corridor. (Fighting for breath may not be quite the right thing to say in connection with sea-fish, but you know what I mean.)

'Upon the scene of these alarms and explanations arrived Mr Seth-Smith, Junior, fresh from a cheery gathering of medical students. Without waiting to change from evening dress he hurried to the scene of the trouble.

'The powerful electric lights had been switched on to the wreckage. The homeless tenants of the tank writhed about on the floor. Dog-fish snapped at his ankles—poorly protected with dancing pumps—while huge congers barked with rage. (It would seem as if it were the dogfish which *should* have barked, but we must stick to the truth.)

'The work of saving the lives of the fish was made difficult and dangerous by the shattered pieces of inch-and-a-quarter plate glass which lay about. One chunk, which was too heavy to lift, had been hurled for 15 yards. The thermometer of the tank was found 75 feet away—astonishing testimony to the enormous pressure exerted by 7,000 gallons of water, weighing more than thirty tons.

'But there was the rescue work to be done—fish were flapping their lives away, and so there was a rush for big hand-nets and a search for alternative accommodation.'

*The Hidden Zoo, by Leslie G. Mainland, 1925*

The Gorilla House, designed by Lubetkin in 1932

## The Gorilla House
'NEW GORILLA HOUSE ... the Council, after the purchase of a very fine pair of young gorillas in August, decided to arrange for the construction of a new house suitable for gorillas or other large anthropoid apes ...

'Mr B. Lubetkin, a Russian architect of the British firm, Messrs Tecton, Ltd, solved the problem in a brilliant fashion. He designed a circular house, divided into a northern portion as the permanent quarters for the apes and a southern half which is an open-air cage. A revolving metal screen is concealed behind the northern half when the cage is open, but by a gearing can be revolved in a few minutes so as to close the cage and transform it into a hall for visitors. The northern half is constructed in reinforced concrete with a lining of cellular concrete which has high insulating qualities. Cork insulation in the roof prevents condensation and economizes heat. It is lighted by a clerestory window admitting the maximum of winter sun. Heating and ventilation are carried out by an air-conditioning plant which washes the air free from fog, dust and germs, humidifies it and sets it in motion at the rate of fifty feet a minute ...'
*Annual Report, 1932*

## Further thoughts on a country zoo
'Regent's Park, on a clay soil, in the smoky atmosphere of a great city, can never be an ideal place for animals, and there have been rumours and suggestions as to the transplantation of the Zoological Gardens to a locality with fewer disadvantages. Such rumours, for the present at least, may be dismissed. So long as the Society derives its income from Fellows and the public, the Gardens must be as near central London as possible; and even if the large sum required for laying out new ground and erecting new buildings could be obtained, and if permission were granted, there would be no great advantage in moving to another of the London parks, whilst transference to Richmond Park, the Crystal Palace, or somewhere near Hampstead or Highgate would be a dangerous experiment financially, and no great gain from the point of view of soil and climate. But there is an alternative that the Society no doubt will bear in mind. There is still cheap and good land to be obtained within twenty or thirty miles of London. The Society ought to acquire several hundred acres of such land and gradually develop it, not as a zoological exhibition for visitors, but as a farm for growing suitable food and a

[149]

breeding and recuperating ground for animals ...'
*Saturday Review, 'The future of the Zoological Society',
by P.Chalmers Mitchell, 28 August 1909*

The site is purchased
'The Council decided in principle that it would be to the advantage
of the Society to invest part of its reserve funds in the purchase of
freehold land, if a site suitable for ultimate development into a
Zoological Park could be obtained. In December, the Hall Farm,
Whipsnade, was inspected and approved by the Council, and it was
agreed to negotiate for its purchase.'
*Annual Report, 1926*

'Considerable progress has been made with the transformation of
the Society's estate of 500 acres at Whipsnade into a Zoological
Park ...

'The scheme under which the Ministry of Labour supplied 150
men from distressed areas has worked to the satisfaction of the
Ministry and to the advantage of the Society. The Ministry paid
three-quarters of the cost and seconded one of their own staff to
supervise. The men were changed at intervals of two months; with
a very few exceptions they improved very rapidly in health, took to
the work well, and a large proportion of them after their stay with us
obtained regular employment on commercial terms. They were
engaged chiefly on road-making, quarrying chalk and gravel, and in
wet weather, rough carpentry.

'During the year over three miles of internal roads have been
made and footpaths got ready. Four chalk-pits have been excavated,
the material being used for road making; the pits have been shaped
so that they will make dens for large carnivora when there are sufficient
funds to render the walls secure from weathering ...

'In the development of Whipsnade Park every effort is being made
to preserve and improve the natural amenities of a very beautiful
district. Although it is to be a Zoological Park containing wild animals,
great care is being taken to make it a sanctuary for British wild birds
and the flowers, trees and shrubs natural to the region. It is hoped
that it will attract not only those interested in animals but the even
greater numbers of the public who take pleasure in the beauties of
rural England.'
*Annual Report, 1930*

The first keeper moves in
'It was also agreed to appoint A. Macdonald, first-class keeper in charge of pheasants, to be, for the present, Keeper in Charge of Whipsnade with the occupation of the new lodge at the Whipsnade gate when it was ready.'
*Minutes, 18 September 1929*

'WHIPSNADE BESIEGED. Overwhelming rush of people to the new open-air zoo. Traffic facilities break down. Railway bookings from London to Luton cancelled. For the first time for many years, railway bookings from London were suspended by order of the police authorities.

'The bookings in question were from London to Luton, and the trouble was caused by the great popularity of the new open-air Zoo at Whipsnade.'
*Morning Post, 26 May 1931*

The Penguin Pond at Regent's Park
'The new Penguin Pond, referred to in the Report for 1933, paragraph 34, was duly completed in time for Whitsuntide. It is constructed in modern reinforced concrete, and the architects, Messrs Tecton, have taken full advantage of the plastic possibilities of the material. Without doubt it has proved extremely satisfactory for the penguins, and has the advantage of being easy to keep thoroughly clean. The general public have shown their appreciation of it by making it one of the most popular exhibits in the Gardens. As always happens in the case of new forms of artistic beauty, there have been unfavourable criticisms, but it has received great and flattering attention in technical architectural publications in this country, Europe and America, and the Society has been congratulated as a pioneer in artistic and practical architecture.'
*Annual Report, 1934*

Pets' Corner
(Now the Children's Zoo)
'During the summer, a new type of attraction was added to the gardens in Regent's Park, in the shape of the enclosure on the old Fellows' Lawn which was at once popularly christened "Pets' Corner". In this, a number of animals were kept which were tame enough to be handled by the public. They included a young chimpanzee, a lion

The Penguin Pond at Regent's Park

cub, a Shetland pony, a small python, a baby yak, a young eland, and a giant tortoise, some rabbits, young pigs, etc. Visitors were admitted to the enclosure on payment of one shilling. For this they were entitled not only to make friends with the animals, but to be photographed with whichever of them they preferred. They were also allowed a near view of the Chimpanzee's Tea Party, which took place every fine afternoon at five fifteen in a cage in the centre of the enclosure. The Pets' Corner proved very popular, 6,918 visitors paying for admission during the three months during which it remained open. Of these 4,332 were photographed; by far the greater number elected to be photographed with the chimpanzee, the lion cub being a rather poor second.'
*Annual Report, 1935*

[152]

After the Second World War the Society started an extensive pro-gramme of redevelopment, the driving force from the mid-1950s being the Secretary, Sir Solly (now Lord) Zuckerman. New stores, workshops, garages and an animal Hospital were built in 1955–60, the Cotton Terraces in 1963, and in 1964 ...

The Snowdon Aviary

'By the end of the year the Northern Aviary [now the Snowdon Aviary] was complete except for final adjustments to the wire mesh, and the planting and landscaping of the surrounding area which it was hoped to finish in the spring. To provide seats for visitors there is a long shelter, which is divided by open pergolas into four bays. Pictorial display panels giving general information about birds are being prepared for the walls of this shelter.'

*Annual Report, 1964*

The new Elephant and Rhinoceros Pavilion
'The completion of this building, which will house two African and
two Indian elephants, and four rhinoceroses, is an important step in
the redevelopment programme ... In their new house the elephants
will enjoy modern facilities, including a sandpit, outdoor and indoor
bathing pools (the latter heated), special heating and ventilation of
their dens, and a spare den for use as a sick bay. The rhinoceroses
also have a sick bay and a "wallow" in their paddock.'
*Annual Report, 1964*

This was followed in 1967 by the Charles Clore Pavilion for Small
Mammals which includes a section with artificial twilight so that
nocturnal animals are active during visiting hours.

In 1972 the Society's fine collection of primates was re-housed in
the Sobell Pavilions for Apes and Monkeys, a group of buildings
designed by John Toovey that give a choice of protection during bad
weather and open-air freedom in good weather. At the present time
the old Lion House of 1875 is being replaced by a vast complex of
imaginatively designed enclosures for the larger cats which is due for
completion in spring 1976.

The Sobell Pavilions for Monkeys and Apes were designed
by John Toovey and opened in 1972

# EPILOGUE

After its first one hundred and fifty years, the Zoological Society is as active as ever. Its fine collections of animals at Regent's Park and Whipsnade provide material for much research in the fields of taxonomy, comparative anatomy and physiology, human and veterinary medicine, pathology, ecology and animal behaviour.

But while remaining true to the Society's original scientific and educational aims, the Zoo has given so much pleasure to successive generations of visitors, that it now has an equally well-established social function. To be able to retreat to the Gardens and observe such a variety of animals is both psychologically and sociologically important for man. It enables him to keep in touch with behaviour patterns and to be aware of the interdependence of all things in the natural world.

' "I have found the Zoological Gardens of service to many of my patients. I should prescribe for Mr Pontifex a course of the larger mammals. Don't let him think he is taking them medicinally, but let him go to their house twice a week for a fortnight, and stay with the hippopotamus, the rhinoceros, and the elephants, till they begin to bore him. I find these beasts do my patients more good than any others. The monkeys are not a wide enough cross; they do not stimulate sufficiently. The larger carnivora are unsympathetic. The reptiles are worse than useless, and the marsupials are not much better. Birds again, except parrots, are not very beneficial; he may look at them now and again, but with the elephants and the pig tribe generally he should mix just now as freely as possible.

' "Then, you know, to prevent monotony I should send him, say, to morning service at the Abbey before he goes. He need not stay longer than the *Te Deum*. I don't know why, but *Jubilates* are seldom satisfactory. Just let him look in at the Abbey, and sit quietly in Poets' Corner till the main part of the music is over. Let him do this two or three times, not more, before he goes to the Zoo.

' "Then next day send him down to Gravesend by boat. By all means let him go to the theatres in the evenings—and then let him come to me again in a fortnight."

'Had the doctor been less eminent in his profession I should have doubted whether he was in earnest, but I knew him to be a man of business who would neither waste his own time nor that of his patients. As soon as we were out of the house we took a cab to Regent's Park, and spent a couple of hours in sauntering round the different houses. Perhaps it was on account of what the doctor had told me, but I certainly became aware of a feeling I had never experienced before. I mean that I was receiving an influx of new life, or deriving new ways of looking at life—which is the same thing— by the process. I found the doctor quite right in his estimate of the larger mammals as the ones which on the whole were most beneficial, and observed that Ernest, who had heard nothing of what the doctor had said to me, lingered instinctively in front of them. As for the elephants, especially the baby elephant, he seemed to be drinking in large draughts of their lives to the recreation and regeneration of his own.

'We dined in the gardens, and I noticed with pleasure that Ernest's appetite was already improved. Since this time, whenever I have been a little out of sorts myself I have at once gone up to Regent's Park, and have invariably been benefited. I mention this here in the hope that some one or other of my readers may find the hint a useful one.'

*The Way of All Flesh, by Samuel Butler, 1903*

# INDEX